# Poetic Injustices in AmeriKKKa

## Vol. 2: Justice Denied, Versified

## By

# Coolgmack

**ISBN:** 979-8-9930046-3-1
**Published in the United States.**
**Cover design and layout by Coolgmack**

**Contact/Website:** Coolgmack.com    coolgmack@gmail.com
@coolgmack on all platforms

# Disclaimer:

To whom it may be concerned. The purpose for this book is to stop the burns and for our tots to learn. For them to not return and to encourage them to yearn for a better turn and not be consecutively competitive to earn an urn. As I churn these words into vivid visions reminiscent of the horrid, horrific predicaments that I was positioned in. Growing up in Amerikkka and being a citizen in a country that was different from what the textbooks were mentioning. The intellectual crooks were forcing me to read so I could succeed in a school system that was missing the peace that I needed to achieve. They didn't teach me to be financially free, independently, without the GUV. My apologies, I was just a product of the streets.

But I am not a racist! Nor do I promote hatred towards Caucasian races that operated and slave-traded my ancestors and my generation. I'm just against injustices. It's just us against this racist systematic government, and the instilling of the Willie Lynch philosophies, which is the linchpin to the white supremacy missions. It's US against THEM. Which "THEM" can be members of any race that implements hate. So, if it doesn't apply, then let it fly; and if it does, then shame on you. It doesn't matter if you're black, white, blue, Asian, or Spanish. I'm against whoever promotes hatred and the action and the planning of it. The only way we can conquer this is with love, knowledge, wisdom, and understanding. It's 2025; we must come together to see the grey area and expand it. We shouldn't hate the next man or woman because of their skin blend. Whether we agree or disagree, we can at least agree to disagree, and let's make this make sense. All lives can't matter if Black lives isn't a matter. We must first reverse the hurt if equality is what we're after.

We must endorse just enforcement in enormous proportions and, of course, get retribution for our losses to offset this awfulness. Education is the key. Don't blame me, I'm just a messenger who cares, prophesizing the truth here, something like a soothsayer. But this isn't a game, this is all truth and dares. The proof is clear, like the last two years. I'm just helping my people with my 20/20 vision through the peephole, so we can be equal and won't see a sequel: Ezekiel 39:27. But I'm not a reverend nor am I half-stepping. These are my God's gifts and methods. I am not a racist. I promote love over hatred and demote drugs for education. This is just my perception from the knowledge I ingested, and my personal experiences manifested, and this is directed to those that selected to infect us. This is for those affected by Amerikkka. God bless US. The author assumes no responsibility or liability for any errors or omissions in the content of this project. The information contained in this book is provided on an intellectual basis with no guarantees of completeness, accuracy, usefulness, or timeliness. Enjoy, live, and learn from this, but do me one favor: let's not look back and turn into bricks, like Lot's wife. Let's use our God-given rights, and that's the will to choose to live life just right. The material and information contained in this book is for general purposes only. You should not rely on content in this book as a basis for making any irrational decisions. Together we will survive. Apart we will demise. Injustice in one city is an injustice for the whole country inside. MLK had a dream, Malcolm had an M16, Huey P had a team. What we have now is distraction, chaos, mischief, and political morphine. There are more teens getting killed, more Black blood getting spilt, more men wearing kilts. Promises not being fulfilled, but it's up to US to keep it trill. Together we stand, divided we fall. This is my act of war that I'm providing for all.

# Dedication and Acknowledgments

For every hand that steadied mine, for every word that lit the way, for patience given, time by time, for faith that never went astray—I acknowledge all my soldiers in this amerikkkan war, especially the ones locked up behind the wall, your spirits unbroken, your hearts still roar, though the system tried to make you fall. To the youth: let your mind outweigh the nine, don't let emotion cloud your brilliance, your shine—one moment of reaction, one unintelligent choice, can silence forever your powerful voice. To my brothers and sisters crushed by systemic weight, victims of racism, of poverty, of manufactured hate—hold your head high, use your mind over matter, don't let substances numb you, don't let your dreams scatter. The vices they offer are chains in disguise, they profit from your pain, from your anguished cries—you're helping them help themselves when you turn to their cure, your strength is the weapon, your clarity pure. To my Caucasians and Asians who fight by our side, together we're mighty, together we rise—racism is learned, not written in bone, we are not enemies, though they'd have us alone. Race is division, a tool of control, there's only one race: the human soul. We need not hate what we don't understand, we can reach out, listen, and offer our hand. And a special message to those who hold power, who judge us by color in their ivory tower—judges and cops who sleep sound at night after destroying a man, his family, his light. False charges and sentences, unjust and long, you're murderers too, though you claim you're not wrong. You envy the spirit you try to contain, but our will can't be broken by your bias and chains. This world is ours, built on struggle and pain, for none who dream can dream in vain. We rise on shoulders, break every bow, and harvest the justice that must be sown. So here, with gratitude and fire combined, I honor those fighting, those left behind: we are lifted from the ground by those who choose to speak the truth out loud. And to all my poets from NYC to LA, let your spoken word rise above the concrete and the truth that you speak overcome defeat.

# Chapter 1: School's in Recession

# Spiritual Immortal Combat

It's the return of COOL-G-MACK-ALYPSE. I know how long that y'all have been waiting, but I'm back at this poetry in motion motivation. spitting facts that crack that myth while cultivating.it's for you to stay focused and patient, while opening your mental renaissance. Let freedome ring ☝. I'm a king and a pro black activist wreaking havoc to uncivilized savages. I'm against any white supremacists and them fascist pricks that's trying to stick chips in our fingers so they can pick US apart fast as a whiff. but I'm gifted with art, so I'm going to do my part expressing with my heart, so we don't go back to whipping them whips. I'm guarded with God à la Allah and I bear witness to him. I ain't the one who started it but I will help finish them. This spiritual immortal combat is never ending, them devils are relentless, so we must do whatever we gotta do to defend against them, there's no room for racism in this un-united nation of independence. Which is filled with plagiarism and unfavortism to the brown skin indigents. This goes for the racist judges on them benches that love to mass incarcerate black men and give them unfair sentences. in their coded compositions that are too long for their comprehension, which is kinda senseless that we don't pay attention to this.

Why are their hearts filled with this vindictiveness? Why do they bear false witness on Jehovah's blemished images? Why do they attack His lineages, and in their judicial compartment syndicates they join forces against the millenniums? whose undivided attention is deficient because of the electrical distractions that leaves them inefficient and passionless. They won't stop until everyone of us is a felon and/or in a prison. stop snitching, telling is only helping them fill up their detention centers. Let me not forget to mention their intentions of brown men, women & children in an unauthentic division. but if you ask us if their mathematician has glitches their mathematics doesn't add up, that's why they rather divide and subtract us (that's a fact bruh!) Watch how they distract us with entertainment & fake news on tell-lie-vision to keep US enthused and capture our views with subscriptions. Are you even comprehending this? Are you even listening? Comprehension is the essentialism to wisdom retention conditioning. In other news they don't want you to discover the pews but they'll use your talents to fill up their stadiums. A 20/80 percent cut is how they are paying them, playing them. using them, then trading them. They never want us to be independent or for us even to mention this. I can't be okay with this black exploitation viciousness in my vision lenses. So I came to shed light with the truth, cut at the root, gut out the bad fruit if that's what I have to do, to get rid of that black soot. With facts and proofs that's my task and my route I'm my poetic happiness pursuit. I do this for the culture, I do this for the youth, I do it for our past, I do this for the present and I do this for our future. Physically, slavery allegedly has been over but we still can't recoup from the lost soldiers and being crossed over like Jehovah. The government will still keep us hanging like Mr. Cooper while we are in the midst of a stupor, that's why education is so imperative for Us to move up. We can't accept what we've been used to, being used up, then tricked and confused by her... mrs. Amerikkka. we have to force a legislative change for us to improve to better things or else that liberty bell may never ring. If we were to just sit there praying and waiting for heaven to rain, it'll never reign so You have to stay ready like when tevin sang. Nearly everything we were taught in school were lies, just opinions of guys that could only see through their racist unapologetic eyes, but now we're awoke and wise And I'm stillmatic now, I can see the dead birds flying through the broken skies. They're slick with their disguise and quick to come up with gimmick equations like depopulation control and inflation during the plandemic manipulation. They want US to take our lives for granted or vacate it by taking illogical mental health vacations in higher elevations. They'll wait with patience to germinate the bad seeds that they planted to see the repercussions from the fruitions of the vegetation famines. They'll stay up all day just to break knights in an unrighteous heist like some type of sacrificial lamb or goat. Whether it's physical, spiritual or it's financial, their harmful ways are almost always substantial. If we don't stand up to them and plan for our freedom we will just accept the consequences at a per diem. We can't join them so we gotta beat 'em and teach them a lesson, then recede them, that is our only hope for our freedom's progression. I am not a reverend but I came to preach this testament on behalf of my past brethren who couldn't foresee the overseer's regimen detriments. For yet our 40 acres and a mule settlement hasn't been met, they just took the land and embezzled it then left us in debt. then swept it under a rug then gave us the rest of the pork barrels and all we could say was no bro and yes pharaoh. Is it the right wing or is it the left wing we have to accuse, but what are we to do when the whole damned bird got the flu, with 3 vaccines to use they are asking you to choose but blacking out the rules, leaving the blacks bruised with the blues. We sure can't leave it to dr Fraudchi or willie gates to depopulate our states or congress to inflate our fate or wait on faith. They already gas gauged and boosted the urban crime rates, which has no effect on the affluent and the suburban tristate.

It's 2025 so how in the NRA are they getting all these guns on the streets to these teens, who are dying mad young, buying drugs. Running around like thugs reenacting Fortnite, their TVs need to be unplugged. Don't get caught up at night, by a slug from an assault rifle legally bought in a gun store with a price which doesn't suffice the consequences that's being paid for. But It's all about the Benjamin's and the benefits but if we unite and fight this unrighteousness we can win this.

# Math

Are people forgetting about the wars? Especially the two longest ones in huemanity's cause. Since the dawn of existence, it's been written in blood and flawed laws. Still raging on—good vs evil, Black men vs the world and her claws. We're still captives—I mean captivating—by the applause 👋 Fascinated by fame while they fabricate our flaws. Massive cash 💰 it's making, faster than Congress can make it and pause, to send billions overseas, while our babies sleep on floors

Passive wages to our nations while backing inflation gentrification stations. They are trying to erase our foundation.  Escalating to a wider and higher vibration that reverberates through your ears 👂 in silent sedation. E-commerce, erasure, evasions. Through your TVs 📺, androids 📱 , and coded sensations. They're erasing our stories, replacing our stations with algorithms that feed your fears and temptations. But I see through the smoke, through the veil of the distractions. Through the TikTok dances and the Instagram captions. Through the news cycles spinning manufactured reactions. While they are privatizing prisons and monetizing our women and our interactions and inactions.

You have to replace it—freedome + knowledge + wisdom = 7. That's divine math, a sacred path, and a universal lesson. Do the mathematics, it's basic, No guessing. Seven chakras, seven seals, seven heavens-- seven scripts, seven stages of brain development.

So, I meditate in silence and elevate through defiance. Break the chains of compliance and build a mental alliance. I know the science, with ancestors whispering truth silently. Their spirits riot in me—I'm the storm, not the one that walks off quietly.

# Division by Design

Biden just let five thousand immigrants in NYC
Now times ✖that by 3 for the rate that they breed
Niggas like you and me are becoming impurities.
So, you better get right with whom you believe--in
Because the disparities weren't already even ⚖️

HIStory keeps repeating
Because niggas acting like they don't see it
Reverting to the King James Version of Jesus
Turning their cheeks in
It's mind-blowing 🐺, knowing
the knowledge that we keep in…
The tombs 🪦

While we're chasing wounded wombs 🐿
Trying to be goons 🔫 but looking like raccoons 🦝

Savages and scavengers
scamming on the next passenger's loot
The passion of the past massacres is passing us
cuz
Vroom 🏎

We're all family in the tree 🌲 of life.
One sun, one moon.
If you're reading 📖 it right.
See 🔎 what I write, stay tuned 😵‍💫
Complexion is just a division of one's discretion
Don't cloud your visions with their intellectual
weapons... boom 💥
Drugs and television 📺-- duh 😒
That's not really reality-- bruh 😵
They're using your proprieties to generate a salary
To be aware is to be alive
To be alive is to open your eyes and see
Stay awake and take it 1 day at a time
Stay on the grind. Elevate your mind.

# Disconnected

The system has double standards—they swing first, call 911 second, and then act like victims when you reckon with reckless disrespectfulness. The violence beckoned, but you stand alone. Constantly lonely though never truly alone, you have divine protection in your bones, royalty that's been overthrown but never broken, never cloned. Never sulking. Never condoned.

While they peep through their screens, scrolling through their manufactured dreams. The dopamine hits and laser beams of blue light hijacks their schemes-- of ever waking up, to see the matrix isn't what it seems. One hit isn't enough. Their brains on pause, their thoughts on lease, algorithms got them on their knees while they think they're at ease—the real pandemic is this disease of disconnection from their inner peace, from self-perception.

The irony cuts deep: they consume the culture like vultures. Bumping our beats, repeating what goes on in the streets in every tweet. The dumb, deaf miss the message underneath the heat. They want the aesthetic, not the truth—the vibe without the proof, the sound without the booth. That's where pain gets recorded, where youth get distorted by systems that have been hoarded by those who can afford it.

Can't we all get along? That's the question for the ages, written on these digital pages, while the real war rages—not in the streets, but in the cages of our minds, enslaved by Wi-Fi waves and minimum wages. See how time flies?

Wake up. The king never knelt, and the truth you always felt is the hand you've been dealt—play it right, keep your shield tight, stay in God's light and out of the limelight.

# Swim or Sink

When I was young, my parents left me to the wind.
They pushed me into the ocean and said,
"Turn around and swim."
That's what I did, though I was truly scared.
I kept kicking and swimming,
even though I was unprepared.
Now I'm here. I made it out of the water.
I didn't get life's goals from what it had to offer.

If I had my wish, it wouldn't be wealth.
It would be for us to love each other
and to love ourselves.
My mom did her best.
She would hug me and kiss me.
Our crib was infested;
it seems like I've seen more mice than Disney.
Fried pork chops, mac and cheese
messed up my kidneys.
Every other day, it was either Mickey D's or
Wendy's.

When I grew older, my heart turned colder.
I was surrounded by either rats or king cobras.
But still, I persevered.
What's worse than tears,
is living life like the end of the earth is here.

I must have broken a thousand mirrors.
I have mad bad luck.
Inferior,
I stayed in trouble trying to reach those fast bucks.
I hustled just to pay the consequences.
It's not worth it.
Experience is the best teacher;
you'd better learn quick.

Learn from my mistakes.
Don't return to that bait.
Stand firm in your faith,
and in turn, you'll be great.

**Young Kings and Queens, listen close to me**,
**This is a plea:**
The world will still push you into the turbulent sea.
The sharks will still circle, the current will pull,
But you are not a victim; your spirit is full.
Let your conscience be free.

# Truth for the Youth

This is my truth for the youth
Take these seeds, cultivate them to fruits,
Pursue prosperity that's long overdue,
And do all the things that influence you
To move through those subdued igloos,
Cold traps that prove to move you
In directions you'd never knew

If you never encountered
Do you, the laws are imbalanced.
Those cowards are empowered by violence
Silenced throughout your childhood.
But with God it's all good

You were distracted.
Your Schoolbooks—redacted.
Facts flipped backwards,
To make you think your enslavers were
masters
We were enslaved to translated biblical
passages
that made it all hazardous,
They called us Black bastards.

But in reality
The so-called forefathers, showed no affection
They were just slave masters of deception.
Using constitutions to futuristically unarm our weapons
With law aggression and amendments that regresses
Now class is in recession.
There's is no progressing,
If we can't get it. And unite for our successes
Knowledge is infinite and time is money.
Be careful how you're spending it.
Because your mind is hungry

# AmeriKKKa Express

Sugar-free ain't sugar-free,
It's still fifty grams of calories
Artificial sugar rushin' through your arteries,
Fats and carbs stackin' — negative energy,
Don't let 'em trick you, do the Knowledge, and read
Between the fine print in the recipe.
Might as well, chef you own sweets
The old-fashioned way, or eat some kelp
Instead of payin' for them retreats,
Invest in yourself, don't mistreat your health.
Treat yourself to a hotel, a suite
Before you defeat yourself,
Ritz crackers gonna tax your wealth.
Hazardous, that's ass-backwards.
You don't need to ask for your master's
Be free, break food addiction dependency.

And please don't mention me in the White House,
'cause they'll flip it — and give me a century,
Of months in the big house, for running my mouth
Reverse the morgue, life off pause,
False charges, by AmeriKKKa Express

My black trump card maxed out,
And they won't let me cash out.
I'm stressed
No stimulus, just gimmicks,
Uncle Sam and Uncle Tom in big businesses,
Brothers undercover discoverin'
Truths they've been smotherin'.
While you were asleep 😴,
They were smuggling in immigrants,
Every other week
I'm not a Republican, not a Democrat,
I'm a Dominican that's black, of African descent,
But to them?
Still just a nigger with no consent.
With a big.... Clip
Slave emblems on my Benjamins,
I keep it 110 percent,
For my God-driven women,
And my God-driven men.
We were heaven sent to win

## What I Made It Through (So You Don't Have To)

I came up broke, broken, and hard
where hope gets stolen in your own backyard.
Where the loudest dreams get silenced quick,
and survival means knowing every trick.
I've danced with danger, slept with doubt,
Seeing the police try to bleed me out.
But I made it through—not just to boast,
But to give this game to those who need it most.

So, to the youth.
Don't chase a path just 'cause it glows,
Don't let poverty define your truth.
If it leads to chains or locked-up doors.
Don't believe without seeing proof
I've worn the bruise I paid the price,
Lost lots of good friends and years of life.
But pain taught me lessons, school won't teach
By God's grace, I made it here so you can receive.
You ain't gotta fall just to feel the pain,
You can learn from me and still win the game.
Use my scars like steppingstones,
So, you can rise with the strength of your own.
Education ain't just in books or in the grades
It's learning to cut through smoke and blades.

It's knowing your worth in a world that lies,
And keeping your truth when the system denies
They'll sell you dreams wrapped up in chains,
they call it freedom, but it feeds you pain.
They'll suit up laws to steal your rights,
And punish you for trying to peacefully fight.

But listen— you are not what they expect.
You are wisdom, muscle, soul, and intellect.
You are the page that they can't erase,
The future's fire, the saving grace.

So don't walk blind... walk bold, walk smart.
Let purpose guide you, both mind and heart.
Read between the lines, question the script,
Flip every trap. If it's not real right might be a trick.
I made it out. But not alone
I had to build back up with flesh and bone.
Now I reach back, my hand extended with truth
So, the path is clearer... because I do this for you.

The time is now, and the power is yours
To break the cycle and open new doors.
You can be the story that they never will tell,
The youth who rose, never went to jail
But it still rose so well.

# Breaking the Cycle

If it weren't for the storms, I wouldn't know the sun,
If it wasn't for bad luck, then I wouldn't have none
If it wasn't for strife, I wouldn't know how to fight.
I have never seen dawn without dancing through the
night.

Been stuck in this tier, but the climbs just begun.
I never ever thought, in here, that I'd see my son
Not just visiting, but standing here, in this cell
This twist I'm witnessing in this county jail
What the helly!!!

I warned him once, I warned him twice,
Told him the streets don't play nice,
But obviously, he didn't take my advice.
I told him the streets may like you, but they don't love.
They'll hug you with heat, then push comes to shove.

I told him my path was paved in pain in the rain,
But he had to walk it; now he's tasting the disdain.
He laughed it off, thought he knew the whole game,
But now he sees that it's more than a name and fame.

But maybe fate had a bigger plan— to show him the fall,
So, he'd learn how to stand... on his own, too, and tall.
Maybe he had to see firsthand what the streets create,
Learn how to be a man, and to appreciate...

To feel the weight that bent my spine,
To walk through that fire that tripped up my mind

Maybe this moment was meant to be,
So, he could witness the cost in me.
So, he could get divorced from the streets,
Learn from the burns that forced me to concede

Maybe this moment's a seed in his chest,
To grow past the curse, to rise and invest.
Not to repeat, but to rise up and above,
To turn the hurt and feelings into love.

Maybe he'll break the cycle and do much more
To break down the cycle and unlock closed doors.
Maybe he will learn, maybe he will teach,
Maybe he will plant new seeds where weeds won't
reach
Maybe he'll build from the rubble that he sees,
Stretch past the limits that I couldn't keep.
And if he does, I will be glad, let it be
I hope that he becomes better than me.
Not bound by chains, but flying free,
Living the life that I dreamed to see.

# Harsh Realities

The game has changed. Nowadays the adolescents are out of lessons—they'll shoot you just for clout. popping Smith & Wesson hammers in front of cameras then running their mouths. Education is redundant in their house. These young guns really be about that murder game without a doubt, playing real-life Fortnite in the daytime with their ladders hanging out their purse pouch. Crouch, shoot first, ouch! Hurt then chirp like a church mouse. IG ID'd their whereabouts. Stray bullets have no name on it when you pull it. Murder rate is to the fullest—most of the beef is over bullsh!t, pun intended, while the rich are using their interest to fund another undercover business. Our interest is in other cryptic crypto riches. I ain't no critic but I'm tired of living in sincere fear that my child might get shot in their rear and/or ear before they even get a chance to finish up their linear school year.

I shouldn't have to wanna move from here, but who cares? This is where I was raised, where I played. I couldn't afford to leave so I stayed. Now I'm made to be a public enemy of the state but I know what time it is... Flavor Flav. But now every day there's gun shots and violence. What is it going to take to stop this unbalance? The block has been challenged. We'll march and rally when a cop kills a black man but turn our head when a black kills another black, damn!!! Fam, where's the equality and accountability? If we don't stop this "us against us" then we really won't be free. These are our harsh realities. Because when one dies, two families cry. It's ridiculous—one's at the funeral, the other is at court getting lifetime sentences. Even if  you never meant it, you can't take back the actions or the facts that you did it with killer intentions. You were just vicious. Now you're in a prison with inhumane conditions, listening to the guards directing you where to shit and piss in. You can't blame the snitches—you put yourself in this predicament. Now your life has just changed in a matter of inches. Now you are just wishing that you weren't in that position, blaming everybody else except your selfish ambitions. You can't accept the man in that mirror to face yourself. You feel inferior—it starts in the interior. It's getting clearer that you played yourself in a movie you apparently appeared as somebody else. Now you're in the cell screaming "somebody help!!"

Now the drugs are clearing up out of your system and you remove the loose toxic toxins. Now you're realizing you had other options and opportunities but you missed them. It took you to get boxed in to return to the majids. 23 hours locked in, is a whole lot of time to reflect and be positive. Now you're watching the scenario replay over and over in your guilty conscience. You were just too conceited to see that the beef was just nonsense, and it all could've been avoided and adjusted. You didn't have to pop him but you shot him out in the open in public. Somebody should have stopped them before it got to the point of this violence. Where were the parents? Where is the understanding.... Silence.

How are all these kids copping guns in the streets which are abundantly cheap? That's the question that is puzzling me.... But shhh 😶 before they put the muzzle on me.

# Mercy over Punishment

I, Coolgmack, do humbly ask the court to
understand
That I am a physically and mentally disabled man.
I do suffer from chronic pain
and a traumatic brain injury,
Which has often, reluctantly, in the past,
Led me to substance abuse and misery.
I'm asking the court for mercy
To give me a treatment program
Instead of jail punishment,
Which will only hurt me. Certainly,
I am willing to do a long-term substance abuse
program.
It took me becoming an old man
To admit that I have a problem.
I won't mess up again, no ma'am.
I understand that in order for me to change,
I must admit that I have a problem
And that my life has become unmanageable.
I must work toward recovery with complete
abstinence
To repair my damaged soul.
I'm too old to be going back and forth to prison,
Incidental to my addiction.
Instead of learning to be a better criminal,

I would like treatment
So, I can yearn to be a better individual
That is my mission, I mean it.
I had a spiritual awakening with God;
I know I learned my lesson.
I'm tired of losing my place of residence
Then coming back home, homeless
In a shelter that is drug infested.
I would like to get my problem corrected,
Then, I will inspire others to recover
through my poetry
And mentor adolescents.
I understand that if I were to mess up
Or leave the program,
There would be severe consequences.
I will, by any means, complete the program
I'm back to my senses.
This time, I will do things different
I will ask for help and take my medicine.
I've learned how to manage my pain
Through prayer and meditation.
I will use poetry and my coping skills
To fight through temptations.
I understand that the narrative of me
Looks bad on paper,
Just like the last violation.
But those charges were dismissed,

And the new ones are without a conviction
I still have the presumption of innocence.
I'm not the violent man that I'm made out to be.
I made some terrible choices, and I admitted it
I was vulnerable and weak.
Please show me mercy.

Since my release,
I've published and authored books
On Amazon and Walmart.
I apologize for my cycle of mishaps.
I'm asking for a fresh start.
When I am focused and sober,
I'm totally a different person.
Please help me help myself
With a treatment program
So, you can see a different version.
Please consider treatment over punishment
in the interest of justice —
So, I can overcome my addiction to substances.

I promise that this will be my last time
Coming to you in handcuffs.
I'm going to man up,
Fight my demons and addiction and stand up.

Thank you for reading this letter/poem.

# Chapter 2: Only in Amerikkka

# Don the Kings

**Only in Amerikkka**
animal's 🐕🐶🦌 got more rights than the Blacks.
Dogs piss on the sidewalk, no fines, no tax.
Deer shit 💩 on the grass, no cop on their back.
Cats scratch a nigga — no cuffs, no trap.

**Only in Amerikkka**
we pay for the slacks,
Congestion tickets are draining our pockets,
justice is off track.
Freedom is the opposite
Lady Liberty laughs,
Banking our struggle, stacking the cash.

You got a strike being black
**Only in Amerikkka**
facts get lost in the sauce,
Truth twisted up, scriptures crisscrossed.
Artificial artifacts packaged as facts,
Deception is art,
And we are the ones being attacked.

**Only in Amerikkka**
Niggas miss the signs,
Lies in disguise got us ditching the lines.
Division in the habitat, subtraction Tubi exact,
The math ain't adding up — it's a system collapse.

**Only in Amerikkka**
They replace us fast,
Immigrants are let in while our future gets slashed.
Causing a collision, a cultural crash 💥,
The movie 🎥 already told us that
The Panther was Black.
They don't want Wakanda rising; they fear that path.
Only in Amerikkka, do they rewrite the past.

**Only in Amerikkka**
They send money away,
While the hood goes hungry every night, every day.
Living with rats 🐀 in a broken-down trap 🪤,

Chasing cheese while they laugh, never giving it
back.

**Only in Amerikkka**
Retribution's erased,
Justice delayed, our history replaced.
You black you can catch a Covid cold 😬
Quicker than a 🚕 taxicab, the truth is undersold.
Refunds are owed for the pain in our backs,
For the crimes of the supremacists, written in black.

**Only in Amerikkka**
Their reign couldn't last —
That crown cracked open,
The future outclassed.

**Only in Amerikkka**
Where the struggle is raw,
But the people still rise,
'Cause we're bigger than the law.

# Obamanation Revelation

They said the Obama-nation
was an abomination to this nation—but how?
He showed and proved what faith
and determination allows.
Yet in this generation, the federation
still caters to racist Caucasians,
despising Blacks, hating Asians
government halls echo Satan's imitation.
We too asleep to see their tactics,
their quiet mathematics,
using us against us with laws that mask the
madness.
It's black and white in our faces—no grayness
a spiritual-political war that's ageless,
older than the flag they wave with shameless pride.
They still hate Obama for what?
Just the sound of his name twists tongues shut.
But they hail Trump?
That term proved this land divided, raw, and racist.
Confederate flags just switched to MAGA hats
how you make America great
when it was born on hate?
That's a Snapple fact.
The stars and stripes, to me are chains in color—
a banner embroidered with civil-injustice clutter.
They modernized the whip into prison monopolies,

corporations trading Black bodies for property.
Every week a new name indicted,
Every night another riot ignited.
The media's delighted
pain televised, justice uninvited.
But the only true fight is enlightenment.
Without the head, the body slides by the waistline
our men doing state time,
playing chess and wasting my mind.
The Earth weakens without the Sun's shine,
you reap what you sow;
wheat grows in summertime.
So I'd rather eat crumbs with the humble
than steaks with the fake
no sense gambling my soul
when the stakes ain't great.
The feds let you shake and bake,
just to take your cake.
They don't investigate;
they invest in Gates and wait
let us annihilate, then watch the fate.
One stray from a TEC
and they connect the dots
now your codes are your ops,
broadcast live at seven o'clock.
Illegal moves make holy men prey,
reverends or not, they'll snatch your day.

When you get locked,
your wife signs her name beside your spot.
It's 2025, and unarmed Blacks still drop
cops stretched with licenses to kill,
Heckler & Kochs primed for the thrill.
We must protect the youth
the fruit of our genealogy truth.
This ain't geometry;
know your geology.
It's simple mathematics
only five percent grasp it,
The rest are still savage.
Guard your mouth, your mind,
your temple, your soul.
You don't have to like me—just listen whole.
For I am one of God's people;
We are not equal in the devil's sequel.
He tricked Eve like Knievel,
split Adam with other evils.
His mission is division—
to steal, kill, destroy with precision.
So, guard your castle, defend your throne,
the devil prowls to claim your home.
Remember this:
His rebellion is endless, his envy relentless.
Only faith, focus, and truth can end this.

# Stone-Faced in AmeriKKKa

Coolgmack — a pro-Black activist and author,
Standing tall against white supremacy
That's a warrior, that's a martyr.
AmeriKKKa still profits off systematic torture,
Designed to keep us tamed, chained by laws that distort us.

I go against the odds, still caution my peers
Your "friends" will be the quickest ones to cross you in tears.
But I'm armed with the Son of God as my sole endorser,
Even when the DOJ tried to lock me and toss the order.
You see me today — stone-faced, unbothered, unmoved.
Not Rushmore — my resolve stays carved in truth.

I don't condone the jakes, I don't trust the law,
'Cause I saw how they built them prisons — designed to
flaw. The OGs that spoke wisdom? The young ones ain't
listenin', Now they tote switches, playin' God in the system.
Trading their souls for a moment of clout, Smokin' K2 spliffs
till their lights burn out. Bodies decayin', livers and kidneys
missin', While corporations profit off their slow-dyin'
existence.

I've seen legends turned into memories, morals made
secondary, Icons fade like murals, names whispered in
cemeteries. Remember Keith — used to play for the Heat?
Got caught in them streets, sprayed by his own peeps. Now
the cycle repeats. Thirteen-year-old, laid cold in the
concrete.

Them strays ain't cheap — they cost two lives apiece,
One dead, one caged, both swallowed by the beast.
Two brown families weep while social networks speak
In monotone grief — another headline, another week.
Keep one eye open, watch who you roll with, stay focused.
'Cause fentanyl laced the smoke, that's a slow-death potion.
Same poison the POTUS promotes in motion
They dose devotion, profit off our emotions.

Before you vote, research their quotes,
Most politicians are puppets, sellin' false hope.
They promise change, then vanish like ghosts,
Jump over our pain like locusts on toast.
Hocus-pocus, political hypnosis
They gave us stimulus checks, then stole our focus.
While they gentrify our blocks, amplify their stocks,
Unified franchises never stopped the plots.

Flooded our corners with racist cops,
Glocks cocked, but no safe spots for our crops.
Won't build schools or jobs for our youth to chill,
But quick to shoot instead of teachin' skills.
Still, I preach, earn legitimate wealth,
Build your worth, build yourself.

Give zakat, make salat, live by will
Do your part for Allah's will.
Through pain, I rise — through struggle, prevail.
I Write my truths in blood, and I will not fail.
Inshallah.

# Grants & Food Stamps

Only in AmeriKKKa, the tables stay twisted,
We get evicted, while the newcomers get assisted.
Only in AmeriKKKa, the plans stay hidden,
We blind and high while they move with precision.
Stop ● look •• and listen ♪ See ◉ for yourself,
open your 3rd ◉ dimension. free your wealth

While brothers on the sidewalk were forced to be a vagrant
Immigrants seeking asylum get kits and donations,
More rights, more benefits, more houses and grants,
While we fight for Section 8, Medicaid, and food stamps

They congest our hoods, and keep us in confusion,
Shipping us to prison while they're building their inclusion.
We watching it happen, the plans in plain sight,
Replacement on the table, but we were too tired to fight.

Only in AmeriKKKa,
They legalized weed, now we are high, the games are did.
Their mi$$ion moves silent, replacing, rearranging.
We the original builders, but they are shifting the vision,
We are losing ground too fast to a long-planned decision.
Evictions, addictions, systemic afflictions,
While they break ground on brand-new subdivisions.
Prison pipelines for US, new grants for them,
They stack their empires while we sink in the system.

# Poly-Tricks ✍🏼

Those acts, the so-called racist signed,
Can get you tricked by politricks if you are blind.
But I be knowing the poly-tricks,
Politicians spitting in hydrographics.
Some don't listen to the opposition;
They like to twist it to fit it, then miss the mission.

But if you know, then you already see
the difference between their stance and reality.
From the pulpits high, they preach their lies,
Pole-splitting truths that they designed in disguise.
It is what it is, and it ain't what it ain't,
the Truth gets smothered in political paint.
Tune in to @itbeewhatitbe,

IG live with facts and ideologies.
Cut through the noise, make the message clear,
Truth for the fake idols, the world needs to hear.
They feed you division on every screen,
Left versus right, red versus green.
But behind closed doors, it's the same old team,
Playing chess with your life selling you a dream.
They sign the bills with a smile and a pen,
Promise you change, then lie to US again.
Same old game, just a different face,
The same old lies in a different place.

You think you're woke 'cause you picked a side?
Both lanes lead to the same demise.
Open your eyes
They keep you beefing with your neighbor next
door,
While they stack paper, asking for more.
Read between the lines, the pattern is clear,
They profit off anger; they feed off fear.

Divide and conquer—the oldest trick,
Keep the people fighting while they get rich quick.
So don't get twisted by the media spins,
Don't let them decide where the truth begins.
Research it yourself, question what you see

That's real freedom--That's sovereignty.
Peace

# Arithmetic of Forgetting

They rise, brick by brick, steel jaws swallow the sky,
while the city forgets its children, walks past them
dry-eyed.
Ever since that thunder—some call it a "plandemic"
some call it an accident, sidewalks turned to altars
where survival makes its stand when Havoc hits.
Blankets fold like prayers, carts roll like ships,
laughter stretched thin on three coins and cracked
lips. The new towers arrive with new gods to salute.
Cold, tall, and smooth, Balconies sipping sunsets
while the streets bear the proof. Inside, chandeliers
glitter, they toast to "progress" made. Outside, a
child maps a broken concrete cascade, naming
ghosts by each shade. Is it a coincidence that

tenements bloom where elevators hum? Or da math of oppression, where the poor get the crumbs? The arch enemy Architects sketch straight lines while our people beg to eat. It's beyond the feed, geometry of struggle, angles sharpened in the street. Cranes swing like metronomes, but they miss the beat, new addresses minted while gentrification peaks.

Meanwhile, drinks pass in backrooms without light, stamps like shields, guarding bodies out of your sight. "Diplomatic immunity" preaches like Jim Jones in the air, but who cares to grant immunity from hunger, from
 Despair? Who gets the keys, and who gets the locks? Who climbs the condos, and who sleeps on the block? I saw a man plant a seed in sidewalk stone, swore it would bloom into wealth, into a home. I saw a mother with six, building cardboard walls, teaching her children love through the holes, though the ceiling still falls.

They trade in small mercies, in crumbs for our breath, while the naked penthouse above glows arrogantly blessed. So, is it a coincidence, or is it by design? Forgetting's not an accident; it's written between the lines. Systems reassign value: glass over grit, permits over people, and profit over spirit.

The truth hits low, on a crate with no shine, niggas sipping bitter coffee, counting nickels for a dime.
I ask the city a question, and it answers in a veil. In ribbon-cut lies, in policies that kill. It gifts cloaks of justice,
but forgets who sewed the seam, streets speak back in resistance, in the stubborn words we dream.
Under cranes and cold halos, our people survive, building a social media community just to stay alive.

Believe in "coincidence" if comfort's what you seek, The shadows of those vaccines preach louder than they speak. Count the bodies at noon, stretched under that shade, fold that stamped paper boat, watch where it wades. Somewhere between ledger and crates lies the choice, somewhere between silence and mayhem, you'll hear the voice.

We are learning new tongues to name what's denied, a city that builds walls while billions are pushed outside. Until then, my poem will keep the street's fire lit, not coincidence—nah, it's a system we must split.

# Artificial Ties, Real Struggles

The glass isn't half full; it won't be okay—that's bull. But I can't be mad at all; we're all gonna fall. That's how gravity pulls. Why I gotta put my mask on. I ain't scared of COVID infections; I eat Vitamin C that gives my immunity extra protection. Why are these folks looking in my direction, crossing the street when they see me at the intersections? Why does it seem like everyone I meet speaks prophetic? The people are only about and out for themselves—it's pathetic. People form social media friendships that are so artificial. Prosthetic. They're always on a scam mission; I can forgive, but I can't forget it. For the fortunate, the fame—their level just sets regular sales records. Skip the games. Show me the money—no ass betting. There are no true commitments; its past recklessness. They'll use barely half of this effort if you ask them for free, but they'll go all out for the ladies or if you flash them some green. It's too cold in New York, but it's too hot in Cali. I'm too old and too short for shorts, and too wise to not set a salary. But maybe they're right—I might need better life management. How can I get a wife when I have issues with contrite abandonment? How can you satisfy your need for luxury when I have issues when you can't contribute to a fundamental? So sometimes you need to learn to just leave me be. If I get angry and have an outburst like a weirdo... I'm a pissedimistic, looking at it in the worst-case scenario. It's like my energy is off and full of negativity. I reject good, and the bad gets the best of me. So maybe it's me... but it's probably them. I can always find something wrong with them, but 95% of people can find a flaw within the system. Maybe I'm a wreck and a mad perfectionist; I can be an expensive designer but find an irregular stitch. Even on Christmas, if it's not a specific gift, I may get offended. But it is what it is. That's why I pray for the best, but I expect the worst. If it's too good to be true, then in the end it's probably gonna hurt. If I already have a felony, then why should I do good? No one is going to hire me. I'm destined for the hood. My whole family is on welfare—so was the generation before. The government doesn't want us to escape; they just keep regenerating the poor. What am I going to do with a 2G stimulus when I have bills that are due? Plus, I need new kicks—what I'mma do? I'mma spend it quick! Besides, who really benefits from the benefits, because the rich are still getting rich. Tax breaks for their businesses! Why in the world would I work a strenuous shift to see them rich, when it's expensive to see a doctor when you're sick with no medical benefits? Why would I let them deduct from my pay for a 401K, getting interest on my interest, but I need that today! It seems like things will never change; it will always be the same. I see the Declaration as just a page—a decoration— for the Capitol, with MAGA flags on their flagpoles. You see light at the end of the tunnel; I see such a black hole. It's never-ending.

# Acrimony, Decoding, Division

What would you do?
If they jumped you and lumped, you
And call the police when you come through?
I know I made dumb moves,
But what does that have to do
With the facts that happened?
When I want to get my retribution
And take action,
They call the precinct and the captains

why, when they see me
They get weakened and seeking help
When it's just me all by myself?

But I ain't never alone
'cause I walk with Jesus
Who is my shield to the throne.
I break bones into pieces.

I've been a king.
I'm awoke to the things
That is lacking in their domes—
I don't know
Maybe it's the MP3s
Or the television
That tells lies to their visions

That they are addicted to
In their own homes.
Or maybe
It's the fear of the unknown,
It's the near drones
That's outside of their comfort zones

It's the addiction to their phones
That's cardiac arresting
All their attention
Or the Mental handcuffs on their medulla
Never gets mentioned in a sentence,
In the ads, that's indirectly infecting
Their retention.

ADD
Add it all up.
It's mathematically terrific
And sadly true
To the scientific hieroglyphics.
Badly used
But they won't hear it
In the lyrics
In their favorite rap/trap songs
That they are hearing.
Can't we all get along?
Why do they fear this?

# Poetic Injustices of AmeriKKKa

Danmmm! Another Black man shot again,
By the opps—nah, I mean the cops again!
Called them himself,
Asked them for help,
Supposed to protect... but he got dealt.
Oxy Moron's, popped him like a Xan
Paralyzed the community below the belt

No reaching hand, just cuffs and pain,
Another name lost in the endless chain.
I overstand why they hid his race,
News reporters with a poker face.

To keep us blind, to keep us guessing,
Another Black family learns a hard lesson.
This is AmeriKKKa—don't get it twisted,
Where our truth gets flipped, remixed, and resisted.

They let Trump stump the cops' funeral grounds,
But he's silent when another Black man's down.
Where was he then, huh? Playing pretend?
At rallies with MAGA flags, while another soul ends.

When our sisters go missing, no national pity,
But Disney profitably promotes them as queens
Trafficked and tossed, yet no conviction.

Only Black skin will face the court's affliction.
Is that a badge... or a MAGA emblem?
The same system that gave me prison chains

Wants to act like they ain't got them bloodstains.
Ignore it, distort it, and tell me that's justice?
Mi$$ liberty sold us out, can't trust that chick
The system is corrupted, the prisons are flooded,
My mugshot posted, my truth rebutted.
The system to make US homeless
Shelters are cluttered.
Sleepwalkers running around domeless

But I'm Thriving, surviving, singing their truth,
Even when justice continues to rob our youth.
This is Poetic Injustices—coming soon,
Not just a poem... It's a rising monsoon.

From AmeriKKKa's wounds, we bring the sounds,
My form is poetry, words unbound
Until truth and justice in every town
Finally comes around.

# Uncle scam

I am not related to Uncle Sam. I'm the original man from the motherland, who has knowledge of self and their political scams. I'm also part of God's subliminal plan to make known the invisible man's plans to get rid of you, but that's only if I can. We were meant to be fruitful & suitable to multiply. Also to be unified with love, peace & happiness, not enslaved & hogtied.

These devils even put the serpent's semen in the heathens, out came the demons with corruption and destructive scheming. Seeking with evil intentions to demonize our existence. They're trying to take our mind state and rape our democracy and independence. Not to mention the redemption for their lack of genetic embellishments, so they rob US of our youth and try to recreate human development

The most dangerous weed in the garden is jealousy among your fellowship; they'll cloud your dreams just for the hell of it. They have devilish ambitions that are passed down thru their generation's chairmanship, just so they can continue to reap the benefits of their hatredness. They did it while trapping our babies on symbolic Slave ships—Federal Greyhounds in BOP terminals, in Oklahoma outbound, you never know, if that's your hearse for your soul. To them is business, never personal.

What they have now is a modernization of their occupations — they are trying to work US to death literally, small cash slash rations as our payments. The cost of living is too high, and chances to survive are pitifully outrageous. It's like they're still subtly making the slaves pave the pavements— with their blood, sweat, and tears for 40 years for a 401k detainment. Then they're selling their souls to the devil, degrading them, but on another level, working but not paying them. While they're killing the running rebels or defaming them.

Then came in the infamous Willie Lynch's statements on how to keep a slave a slave throughout the ages and generations. They do it with division and blue-eyed pie-in-the-sky religions. Let me not forget to mention also the lynching's, hangings, gangbanging and crack/dope epidemics-- and don't forget the PLANdemic. But the biggest gang bang blue — and I ain't talking about the Crips. I'm talking about the cops with glocks with those extended clips, aimed at you. Even though they claimed that they abolished slavery, they just modernized and upgraded it, but it's all the same to me.

They still to this day have our men and women in division and how can we be able to multiply, if most of our men are in prison? Without them and unity, we both can die; they're subtracting the black seed and promoting the demotion of pro-life. They're kidnapping our preteens to abstract the black genes. They even have slave chants and hypnotics through the books and the magazines.

Everything you read you react subconsciously, which attracts bad habits that attack your conscience deeds. And on the radio airwaves, manipulation manifestations, all you're gonna hear on the stations is black-on-black crimes and promotion of prostitution playing.

They even subtly instill the poison into us through the TVs, as well as the movies, videos, and other objects that we see. I guess they have a complex that's inferior, knowing that we are superior, so they try to oppress us because they're really scared of us. But ironically, they'll instill fear in us, then stay clear of us so we can kill each other, then they'll come and appear with the cuffs.

Then, while we're fighting for blocks and ranks like piranhas in a shark tank, which don't even belong to us or anyone else with a dark face, ponder on that. They put us in traps with imitation cheese with no ventilation to breathe, yelling with their trigger fingers, "Freeze!"

Your rights to remain silent are imbalanced because your only help is speaking up for yourself— but your rights remain silenced. In the court of injustice, there's no justice; you get just the ice, then thrown in the bucket or back of the bus quick. Then cuffed to a bench in a racist precinct, then overly questioned and charged, then stripped indecent.

No one would see this, and because of code blue, they won't let you repeat it, like I already told you, and I hope you take heed to this. Amerikkka's biggest gang is the cops that are using the laws as their tools — but it's all gonna unfold soon... stay tuned.

# Prison planned gimmicks

Prison-planned gimmicks are a derision for division.
Propaganda to kill or enslave our men
and women in prison.

For instance, I bet you didn't know
You will always see nuke microwaves
at the height of your genitals
And don't think that's just coincidental.
Frying your sperm and eggs as illogical or
incidental,
By any means their principle
is to diminish our physical and mental,
End us as a whole:

from prison, drugs, lynchings to exhaustion,
To have us killing each other to microwave
abortions.
I Overstand it, but don't get lost in it.
To them one of US surviving is a living abortion

They took the mirrors,
So, you can't have faith in yourself.
When you finally see your reflection,
You don't even know your self-worth.
They say if you look good, you feel good,
But if you don't know how you look,

How are you gonna feel good?
That's part of the process
Of the breaking of a prisoner conquest
Conquer their self-worth, feed them soy to digest
Which can carry a lot of estrogen,
Which can make a man more feminine.
Using food and oppression as their weaponing
Then they have you taking showers right next to
men
And starve us unless we buy stuff from them:
M&Ms, honey buns, ramen noodles and
Entenmann's.
Don't forget to mention
the artificial sugar they're giving them,
Full of aspartame and saccharine
Which causes cancer and dementia
Which also adds to the madness

The system is designed for you to get lost in the
clink
A portion of the proceeds
goes to the FBOP, DOC Inc.
They incorporated it, just another rich tax write-off.
It's quiet time—10 o'clock lights off
They don't want new inspirations
to go inside your mind.

They forbid you to make it-- out this time

5:30 AM awaken for a new day,
But if you sleep late, you'll lose weight,
Find no food in your trays.
The CO— always have a rude display
In a slave/master kind of way,
Using and abusing as they may.
The revolving door for the prisoners of war,
The results from the injustices of the law
They turn five years of probation
Into a lifetime jail stay-cation.
If you are not on point like a cactus,
They will use illegal prosecutorial practices
In the appeals they'll act as if it's just an accident,
But if it's not challenged, they'll leave it as it is.

Don't get caught up in the TV,
That's just a distraction.
Freedom ain't free
Every new prisoner is a subtraction
To the total population.
The census doesn't account for inaccurate
equations.
You have Blacks, Latins, and Asians
Facing unfair sentences for non-violent convictions,
Even ones that's innocent.

The Prison Plan Gimmick.
The Prison Plan Gimmick.

# Chocolate factory

When I say the chocolate factory I ain't talking about no Willy Wonka. Actually, I'm talking about the blacks being packed in the back of Tonkas, shipped to a prison facility unwillingly—this is bonkers, they're really trying to conquer us. This is all part of Uncle Sam and Willie Lynch's system. Once you get in, it's like a rhythm back and forth, circulating hypnotism with division. It's hard to get out of it but easy to get in it, repetitive longer sentences predicaments turning boys into men. I don't know why it's so hard to say goodbye to the pens again. They make friends and amends then get comfortable laying back like the bucket seats of a Benz, while the devils are stealing their time like a thief in the midst. Their family can't even eat, taking heat from the PINS. No payments to child support ever since you wild out in court. You never got caught but you can't win a battle that isn't fought. It's sickening and saddening—so many blacks & Latins giving the oppressors the satisfaction. It's no joke but behind our backs they're laughing. This isn't by any means no accident, black skins coming in back again in a heated repeated cycle of violence and madness.

This is all a part of a long-term plandemic where you are guilty till proven innocent. The court systems are filthy to the indigent. If you have blackish skin, the courts of injustice will welcome you in with a devilish grin, in buildings that're embellished with sin. Denied bail again so they can send you back to the chocolate factory where convicts and the innocents are running fast and not free. Their mentalities get tortured with their physical degrees. They blackened the windows so you can't see the sun, which isn't coincidental but planned to the T. They make it so you can't see your son for weeks while he's being broken down to a compound in the compound consistently—this isn't to be seen.

The Chocolate Factory, the revolving doors of broken souls, crabs in the bucket personalities all trying to climb the molding totem poles. Peter told on Paul, now their households are ruined for vanity and now he's in the hole on the phone demanding money for the commissary. In the streets he was a beast but now he's bummy, rude and hungry for food because he just wanted to be a fool, now he's succumbing to their rules. Fish Fridays consists of imitation fish, just enough for you not to get sick but their best invested dish the supremacists serve is revenge, get hipped!

From the Jim Crow laws to Willie Lynch's hell show, they're giving out perpetual elbows that'll stick in court like Elmer's Velcro but if you're asleep you'll never know. Whether you're rich or poor, you're black!! They'll pack you in the can like a sardine—there's no space for you to breathe, so why not just revolt so you all can just leave?

The FBOP is getting like 6 G's a week, sheesh!! That's modern-day slavery in the belly of the beast. They got the OGs making license plates and military beams. Threats of inability to be free is how they keep the scene serene.

They have the blacks versus the Mexicans and no one is stepping up, then they have the Latin Kings versus the Netas, the Bloods versus the Crips, and the Muslims versus the Christians, Bronx versus Baltimore, etcetera… but nobody versus the oppressors. Their whole policies and ideologies are messed up but they have this whole corruptive justice system that's supposed to correct us??? They're like no sir and yes sir, then going the extra measures to impress her, to which she is just a Miss Amerikkka replica. She is just the pawn that gets advertised to supply eye candy for the con's appetite, an ill-advised Aphrodite as a sacrifice. Just asking for advice or even a goodnight gesture, you'll get ticketed for reckless eyeballing and your good time is messed up.

The texture of the soul is through the eyes, but some men in prison are blind or too far behind chasing their past and good times. You can't be content and satisfied with living sublime. Not only did prison imprison their minds, they were made modern-day slaves working hours for a dime. Their vision of time is hoping to see the calendar bring in the new year—that's new fears, new tears, new desks, new chairs, new tiers, new peers, ranging men from 19 to 93. People still locked up for weed from their teens from 1993 is hysterical hypocrisy to me.

The chocolate factory is where if two get released then it's eight more that are arrested and hauled off from the streets. In there, it's unreal, congested—they got a fresh bedroll and a commissary sheet, an all-in-one egg roll and a cup of saltpeter juice that's too sweet. The chocolate factory is the prison corporations across the nation that got us all lost in the faux sauce of persuasion, which is just another tax-exempt attempt to lock up blacks, Hispanics and Asians. I'm just saying…. This isn't a game that they are playing.

# AmeriKKKa Endless Cycle

They lock brown people up
Because of the color of their skin,
Then they get them—the kins
And the agenda begins
Over and over and over again.
When is this gonna end?
Amerikkka using laws
Of white slavery
To enslave me
They're brazen, it's crazy
How they're taking us, still
To a mountain somewhere
In Hicksville, or Schuylkill,
Trying to kill our hopes and inspiration,
Killing us with bills
In this wretched nation.
All they wanna give us is Nathan's,
But fund wars—what for?
Why is it you're spending it on?
Incentives that only OTHER men get?
It's plain and simple
They keep popping us like pimples
And make us criminals?
This isn't subliminal.
This is in their agendas and principles.
I need a principal and a general

To make this make sense, bro


They write the laws with loaded pens,
Creating cages, not amends
While we fight for our daily bread,
They count the profits from our dread.
Three strikes and you're gone,
Mandatory minimums carry on,
Private prisons need their quota filled
Another generation's--future killed.


They militarize the blocks that we're on,
Schools are crumbling, resources are gone.
They'll fund a tank before a book,
Then wonder why we turn out to be crooks
That fire burning in our eyes,
Refusing to believe their lies.


Over and over and over again,
The same old story, the same old ends
Dress it up in legal speak,
But we see through it, we're not bleak.
They separate the mothers from their sons,
Fathers locked away by the tons,
Families fractured, communities torn,
Another generation of drugs are born
Into this system, cold and cruel,

Using injustice as a tool
To keep us down, to keep us scared,
To make it seem like no one cared.
But we remember, we resist,
We won't be crossed off any list.
We see the pattern, see the plan
Amerikkka's assault
On the brown and black man,
The brown and black woman too,
This ain't nothing false or new.

When is this gonna end?
When will they comprehend?
That you can't cage someone's soul,
Can't break what you don't control.
We rise above your wretched schemes,
Still daring to have big dreams
Despite the weight of all these chains
Our spirits will still remain.

So, keep your Nathan's,
Keep your scraps,
Keep your poverty traps,
We're building something that
You can't see
A future where we're finally free.
Where all huemen is treated equally

# Trumpets blown

Only in Amerikkka, bruh, where they're trying to trump up charges on a bargain—not for true justice, but for political gain driven by the opposite parties. They seek to take a man's freedom for allegedly sleeping with a porn star, labeling a private transaction as professional prostitution, they are going hard. Where is our OnStar to guide us out of this legal and moral confusion? Side bar... how did Giuliani pass the bar?

You can only find this absurd distortion in the cracks of the Constitution, leaving us looking stupid. While a real war is going on inside our communities, But Amerikkka rather deal with intrusion and gives the NYPD immunity. They call him racist; they call him Satan. But who do you believe in the face of this political sanitation? He freed Lil Wayne and Kodak Black, Harry O from Death Row—those are facts. I didn't make this up bro. Take that for your hypocrisy, because this isn't just what hip hop sees. He freed countless brothers in prison with the First Step Act, getting the feds to cut OGs' time in half. But that won't silence the wraths— how can Amerika lock up its own plaintiff? They're trying to lock him up for laws they themselves have corrupted—that's sick. Yet, the government keeps funding wars on other continents. That doesn't make any kind of sense. Right here, my people are drowning in inflation. We have hungry people getting sick with no medication. There's far too much noise to enjoy meditation. They have the audacity to come after me, to arrest me because of my skin's melanin complexity. They are stressing me out by paying tolls to drive in an unsafe place, taxing me to enter a city where I was born in the first place, often with no warning. What a disgrace.

They say global warming is harmless if I'm rich, but I ain't, I'm just a Black man to a cop's Glock itch. I'm just a felon vet to an officer who can't take his knee off my neck. I guess to them, I'm less than a man. They have no respeck. But tomorrow's war won't just be fought overseas—its right here, right in these mean streets. It's in the prisons, in the schools, in the food that we eat— But all we do, is trying to pursue dreams while we're asleep. They distract us with parties and colors on a flag, while both sides cash in checks and laugh. We can't keep on begging systems built on our backs, for handouts and section 8's just to stay on the map. You were born great. Never forget your history, stay awake. We gotta rise, we gotta organize, and take the power back that they claim we lack. But it has to be u n l -verse the opposition that's a fact. The opps can't stop the mission.
Only then will the truth be checked,
Only then will our people get their due respeck.

# A Call for Protection, a Bullet for Thanks

Another Black man shot dead, not by criminals—by cops, popped him in the head. Let that sink in. He called the police on himself, seeking out for protection and help, but got shot reaching for his belt. There was a lack at hand. A lack of humanity. A lack of care. A lack of a plan. A lack of seeing him as human. A lack of empathy that they could understand—I overstand why the news left out his race. They disguise it, bruh, they confuse the narrative, Give then take. Obscuring what's really happening in AmeriKKKa. They let you forget the pattern. The terror in US. Instead, they platform Trump at the funeral of an officer killed in the line of duty—strange priorities for a nation's grief. Meanwhile, where are the repercussions? They vanished from the streets. Is it Disney magic, or are we buying into the Cosby effect—ignore, deny, and distract? Or maybe they want something deeper from US, our kidneys, perhaps, as a metaphor for what they extract. Our sisters come up missing, victims of human trafficking, but the court system only seems interested in convicting Black skin. The badges become an emblem of something else entirely—not protection, but preparation. The code blue morality. Wait a minute. Trump's in the city again. Politically killing whoever isn't his friend. But this country wants to take this and take that. Taking lives. Taking freedom. Taking futures. Killing Blacks like it's their natural AmeriKKKa habitat. How can you ignore that, Miss Justice? Is justice even in the budget, or has the system been corrupted beyond repair? The prisons are flooded with Black and brown bodies—not like Katrina flooded New Orleans, but close enough to compare. Same abandonment. Same disregard. Same armed guards to protect Miss Amerikkka's affairs. Prison—you put me in there, because I was raising Cain, selling the same drugs that you brought into the community in the first place. You flooded our streets, then criminalized our survival. Then censor freedom of speech. Just so you could get Richie off of me— no Lionel. My life is worth nothing to you in this equation, cowards. You made me work for fifty cents an hour, stripped the power from my dollars. The commissary became terrifying after hours, another economy of exploitation behind bars. Working for the government but can't even get a penchant. I hate this relationship of ours. Stop pushing pedestrians onto the train tracks and the water. Cowards hiding behind authority. Stop the violence disguised as law and order. But flowers. flowers to my kings and queens who are thriving despite it all, nah mean. Flowers to those doing their thing, surviving against these odds, refusing to be broken by a system designed to break them, but finding God.

## Next Trick Won't Stick

They cover their badges and names,
To hide the pain —
They put on Niggas in the ☂ rain,
So, they can feel the flames.
Karen in the flesh,
Devil 😈 in the dress 👗.
Still locking Niggas up
For crimes they didn't commit —
I'm stressed.
How Amerikkka keeps getting away...
I dunno 🤷 but I can guess...
Is this racial discrimination in this nation???
Yes!!!!
This country is a me$$.
What other reason than my skin color
I embraced as I was blessed with 😇.
Cops 👮 locked a Nigga up
Knowing he didn't do it —
The crime as they suggested.
But I was out of jail
Before my food 🍚 got digested.
Iron Sheek right and left it 🥊.
Those charges Imma beat
Like Rocky — yesss!! Kiddd.

Like Jason and Freddy,
They trying to kill my dreams 😫
But Imma chef it 🤚.
Like Curry, my vision isn't blurry.
(Ya heard me 🗣 ) I'm on my deen.

Miss Amerikkka is burning 😨,
Smell 👃 da fluorescents 🌞.
I didn't make this 💩 up ⬆️,
Word to the heavens....
Somebody call 📞 the Reverend....
So, he can prey over these peasants.

I'm sharp like Rakim Allah.
And Al Sharpton, if they test it.
I was finessed with intelligence
And an abundance of patience —
So, there's no finessing
Me out of my freedom
Unless they cheat using weapons

He's gonna remain free
Temporarily locked up
Until their next trick,
Which isn't gonna prosper
Because I was made in His image:
Jehovah,
Without a blemish —
So, its swishes ✔ like George Leftwich—of Villanova.
Resentment of these villain soldiers;

I let go and let God —
He shines His wrath on my path,
Gives me hope when things are.
Imma use THEIR negativity energy
To my advantage in a positive way,
Then reverse the hurt
And condemn the sins that got in my way.

# Kracked Liberty

It's the same old script; they just flipped it with a new cast. They label us fast, then blame US for our past. They say freedom rings, but it's just a silent cracked liberty bell. They sell us dreams, then lock us in cells.

Amerikkka tries to play God but forgets the divine. Judges the soul by the body, and their immature minds. If truth is fluid, then why is justice so rigid? If I can choose my gender, why can't I choose my prison?

They twist laws like scriptures, then preach from a bench throne. But when the system's exposed, they leave us alone. So, I mix up the options, confuse their optics. Because if they can play with the truth, then they can forever lock us in boxes. They are targeting the youth.

And maybe that's the lesson: Don't let them teach you who you are. Don't let them keep you mentally with their bars. Because if they can bend reality, then we can bend back and still be free... no liberty, no peace.

## The Audacity of Karen

Wow, Karen got me locked up. Tried to get me shot gunned up. What the f***!!! What was the fuss 🗣 about? Shut ya mouth 👄 😝 😷, Stop ✊ speaking with hostility to a G... ouch! It's gonna hurt you 😟 👩 👆 more than you tried to hurt me, grouch. She deserves a cell, not an Oscar, being comfortable like a couch.

Only in AmeriKKKa they can this keep happening throughout. A country where freedom isn't free, with inflation and greed in large amounts. They expect a reaction, a stereotype to sprout, but thank God I don't react like the image THEY think I'm about. Thank God, I let it slide and not wild out like Nick with a cannon 📹, instead, I pulled the Cannon 📷 out. That's a triple entendre in case you didn't get it with your spouse,

The cell of the jail, the phone's cell, and the lens that now makes the case on the stand. I put the power down, I took the witness stance, I filmed the whole damn scene of her fear-fueled, white-lady trance. You saw me as a threat, a body out of place, so you weaponized your comfort, your privilege, and your race. The manager runs, the police arrive, the siren wails a warning— all because you decided my presence was a trespass on your morning.

But the lens does not lie, the footage is archived truth, a digital bullet against a century of falsehoods and bruised youth. Your comfort is a cage built on my anxiety and sweat, and the world is now watching what you hoped to keep secret.

So go ahead, call the cops. Go ahead, make your plea. The triple-K is woven deep into the fabric of this land, you see. But the camera has broken the cycle of silence they sought, and your name will be the headline for the lesson you never got. You wanted a confrontation, a spectacle of your command. But you just got a viral clip of your privilege exposed, phone in my hand.

# Audacity of Justice

Only in AmeriKKKa
They Lock you up, throw away the key,
Half a key equals a quarter century
That's the unequal math that they feed to me.
Caught between the wrath of weak
and greedy thieves
Why won't they leave me be?

Only in AmeriKKKa,
They punish pain, sell US their lies,
Where are the drugs coming from?
Who is supplying on the sly?
They call it justice,
I call it business—
Slavery flipping, modern-day logistics.
They flood the block with poison,
Then cage the ones who enjoys and employs it
In the hustle they created,
The perpetual cycle premeditated.

Decades for a dime bag,
Families left behind sad,
Kids growing up fatherless,
Mothers working night shifts timeless
Wish I can bring back Len Bias
The Laws written bias,

Profits for the private
Prisons fillin' supremist's pockets
While the streets stay silent.
Politicians in positions
pulpitting
sniffin' lines in the decisions.
Borders wide open for the shipments,
But they blame the hood afflictions
For the addiction.

Meanwhile...
Sentences get stacked like bricks,
Brown lives on layaway,
Decades ticks.
All the good times flies away
How you give a man more time
For a substance
Than a killer who commits the crime
Manslaughter, its corruption

Generational chains,
Washington's with slave names,
Justice blindfolded,
But the system knows your last name.
Century of months—
That's a life in disguise,
Still asking the question:

Who's supplying the supply?

# **Period!**

That's crazy! I know they made that law, as well as others, to disarm US all—pun intended—but I guess they forgot about that chick called Karma. They thought they could harm us with prejudice, systemic laws, and dropping bombs on us. 💣 But Amerikkka forgot, there's a higher power 🙌 who has his own Laws that are made without flaws. Now they're seeking Black votes, but before, they had Jim Crow laws that disabled Black folks to vote. They disarmed them with amendments based on one incident, but now we have kids going to school with guns—and that's legitimate! Terrorizing tax-paying citizens, placing fear in them, homeschooling their children to keep them out of unsafe predicaments.

And because the NRA supports and funds their campaigns, they won't say sh!t to them. But they complain that urban neighborhoods are to blame for the violence in Amerikkka, but they're the ones who are shipping them—as well as the cocaine, the dope, and the bricks they flip. I never met a hood nigga that was a gun manufacturer or a drug chemist 🧑‍🔬, but it hits different when it's hitting them. It went from being a War on Drugs to them trying to put US all on drugs. And when companies like Pfizer and Moderna get charges, it's swept 🧹 under the rugs, but they're quick to sweep our hoods from under us, giving them "fed time" until it's their "bed 🛏 time"—unless they snitch 😶 on their plug 🔌 or on major crimes.

The cycle 🔁 continues for generations with extensions. With all the men in prison, the females become defensive and defenseless. So, hell yeah, I'm offended when I see with my "third eye" all of their tricks that are so vividly intensive. It's US against them, and there's nothing you can show me or tell me to make me think differently. I lived it. I experienced it. If there's no justice, there's no peace until systemic racism ceases... Period!

# Scamdemic

There's no need to panic, we all have a purpose and a mission. We just need to plan it and be determined to win this. This is our planet! Make sure your feet are planted on solid ground with the understanding of the Book of Life— make it a part of your here and now. Because the devil comes like a crook in the night. Even if you took the plight in the walk in faith, don't forget to look to the right. God will provide for you along the way; just push through the fights, even through the longest days. Just pray and have faith — everything will be alright— ok

This is a message to the Black man, whether you were born here on this land or on African sands. Keep open your pineal gland. Even if you're from Japan or Pakistan, you're still a Black man — never forget that, man! Don't let the Willie Lynch syndrome cause divisions; it'll have us against each other, brim with the wrong intentions. But what we really need to do is to get along in these conditions. Exercise your rights to unite— you have my permission. On the radio, the songs will never mention this, because all they're doing is brewing whispers of satanic incidents in increments. The devil is really the one who's profiting off our music, which is filled with lots of shootings, prostituting, and anti-positive influences. The big record companies are involved in the algorithm — how can we prosper as students when the teachers and preachers are filled with embalmed fluid? They're walking dead alive, but still sleeping through the horror music, while the somber COVID patients are laying up in the trauma unit. There's no "I'll be back" like Schwarzenegger in Terminator. Once they put you on that respirator, they're trying to terminate ya. This is my version of purpose— to return the favor. By the way, racism isn't inherited; it's a learned behavior. Think not? Just study the tots— their only concern is nature. They're innocent in this, until they're taught how to discern with hatred.

Hopefully this gets my poetic justice against the government systems that's filled with corruption, that's currently corrupting our women and children to function. The importance is major, but did you see how Trump chumped our mayor, got him cancelled like his bro's show? This isn't a game, but everybody wants to be a player, and if you know, you know. Every day that I wake up, it's another brother being sprayed up or locked up in prison, taken away from US. But we have too many objects in our optics with no contact lenses. It seems like

we can't see through the fog and the nonsense.
Plus, politics is clogging our senses, and the TVs
are telling lies to our vision.

How do you vote for a president if we don't get
treated like residents, and his speech censorship is
offensive and repetitive? I was COVID positive, and
I got the antibodies in my genes, so why in the CDC
do I need a mandated vaccine? That's ridiculous.
It's obvious they want to keep us high and oblivious,
giving us lifetime sentences in this predicament in
Vicious. But I have to remain pious to keep writing
these incidents like Nostradamus did. These are
just my poetic visions in the times that I live in. Just
like in Tuskegee, they want to use us as
experiments, but education keeps you grounded like
the bottom of the pyramid. There is this
depopulation Ponzi-like scamdemic that's insisting
on division. As you can see, there are no more
family tree gatherings at Christmases. Their tactics
are to divide and conquer, meanwhile they're
gentrifying Yonkers. Standing up is the only way that
we can prosper.

# Chapter 3: Streets, Survival & Struggles

# KILLadelphia Pistolvania

Welcome to Killadelphia, Pistolvania, where if you're black, you might get killed because of the other nigga hanging with ya. It's the land of the jailhouse fathers. But if you get out of pocket, their sons will pop ya. The young shorties' bodies are popping up — on 24th and Poplar, and just up the street on 24th and Parish, a carjacking chase led to a barrage of bullets. One hit a baby's carriage.

Killadelphia, where you can be an Uber driver or a Lyft driver and get jacked, and nobody will be helping ya. They extinguish the survivors; anybody can get hit. They aren't shooting just a bullet; they're emptying out full clips. But they won't get the tears lamented when they don't hit who they intended. Just innocent victims get blipped. The violence and murderous shootings are on a rapid rise, expected to surpass last year's city all-time high. Which should come as no surprise to you and me, Because you can get a gun for an ounce of weed, instead of an honest opportunity.

Killadelphia, the land of the goonies and Sunnis. But you can turn on the news at 3. "A cop shot another youth truancy." True indeed. And I can't grasp the understanding of it. The guns are so rampant that they end up in the hands of kids, and I can't just stand here and act as if...

It's okay. A 4-year-old gets shot by a 2-year-old — and "it's an accident"? These guns have got to be deceptively supplanted and supplied, because every other day it's another Black-on-Black homicide. Which is part of a much bigger plan for our demise with gun genocide — for Black men to die. Then our ghetto neighborhoods get gentrified, and private prison businesses strive to keep alive and thrive.

Welcome to Killadelphia, where they walk around strapped, angry, and heartbroken. "They would rather get caught with it than without it" is their slogan. It's hopeless. Oh, ish! Twenty-four people got shot in a 24-hour stretch. Gunfire tragedies to the capacity! Detectives aren't sending a vest, no initial arrest. Surgery doctors aren't getting any rest. CSI is coming to inspect, to find unsigned bullet casings and faces encased with sweat and stress. It's devastating. A mess. Have you ever met Satan? Yes. The adolescents are depressed. There's nothing else left to live for... but death. No one is coming to them to help; they would rather turn the gun on themselves than go to jail like a book on a shelf. That wet got them vexed. Set tripping and getting bent. It's illogical common sense, but most can't honor the consequences.

Welcome to Killadelphia, the city where Brotherly Hate breeds. These shootings are the infused fruition of a poisonous tree. The war in Philly is bigger than Nino Brown, and these gun-toting teens prance in the streets with the extended clips poking in their jeans. It seems there is no better choice than to pack a .38 to feel special. Violence is all they know in the ghetto.

Killadelphia, where you don't have to be in the mix to get hit — ICU, critical condition, even if you're innocent. You'd better kiss your kids like you miss them. On the West End, they are schizing... on demon missions with the Smith & Wesson. On Allegheny, near Kensington, they get it in. You don't have any business being there if you're not a 215 resident. They're "vamping" in Strawberry Mansion. Big Mamas mourn another son who has vanished. Killadelphia is a dangerous planet. The macks ain't jamming.

You can be a civilian or an OG riding on the SEPTA; those young bulls have no respect or love. They're obviously psychologically messed up. What beseeches them? Pure anarchy. Besides, the Percs and Xannies got them feeling invincible. No morals or principles, never went to school at home, no parental figure. They're vicious and hostile individuals, running around in hollowness, fatherless. But they don't have any problems with popping hollow tips and doing a drive-by, sending you to the hospice quick. To them, catching a body is a godly accomplishment. Busting guns gets more acknowledgement and astonishment than a degree in college gets. That's quite obvious. Those pies and piff, plus the opioid crisis, are a big part of it. Amerikkka's plight is to manifest a social crisis. You can find cartridges in the hands of an arsonist. The youngsters are wilding. Zero-tolerance policy isn't going to apprehend any men from Girard Ave to Richard Allen... You would hate to be caught after dark in Love Park. The demons are lurking with Codeine leans, with kerosene in their hearts. So, don't approach him — he's a hot-headed one, or risk getting toasted with a ghost gun. Then they will put the post up. Now they're a Black legend in the House of Corrections, who, by the way, isn't correcting this. Even the old heads are reckless. Youngsters are selecting to shoot innocent victims. Then they are sent to the PICC. Some turn into a chick and Snitch, just to get right back on the block for a minute with a knife and a Glock. Live at six o'clock, another shooting. "I'm confused." Another Ock just got shot??? When is this all going to stop? This psycho cycle? It can't continue. Have there been any "STOP THE VIOLENCE" venues? Let's show what real men do if there's a problem or dispute. The better option is to box it out rather than to shoot. Those orange jumpsuits aren't cute. We're living in a massive mess. I know there's something better than that. They are letting Lewisburg and Holmesburg get the best years out of you. Don't let the lifestyle or the neighborhood get the rest of you or spend the rest of your years inside of a federally funded cell, Schedule II.

Let's take a stand. Let the gunfire escape from our hands, and pick up a book instead, and seek to understand. You have your roots to stand on. It's the other man who works for the Government that's setting us up to hate our own brothers, man! There are vicious, murderous intentions. They've yet to release stress. One sees death, and the other is released to CFCF. We need less violence and more anti-silence for our solutions. Pollution in the forms of hatred, resentment, hellavision, and music. Amerikkka is mass-producing. Your mind is the most dangerous weapon you can use in response.

Put down the guns and use your intellect. Shoot for the stars. Say yes to success. Insha'Allah, you will get blessed by the best of the best... which is Allah.

Don't change because you want to; do it because you got to. **"As-salaam alaykum wa Rahmatullah wa barakatuh."**

# Only in Yonkkkers

**Only in Yonkkkers...** Where they lock you up because a woman said you weren't right. No evidence, no trial—just her word against your life, and suddenly you're guilty before you even speak. Off to the county, next court date in 24 weeks.

**Only in Yonkkkers...** Where the cops beat you down, after arresting you for drugs that the government itself allowed into the community, because they are the plugs to infest us, to test us, to arrest us, to lock up our souls. A cycle designed to destroy what they can't control.

**Only in Yonkkkers...** Where the thots rob you Then call the cops on you, and now suddenly you're facing robbery in the third degree. Facing charges that you somehow stole your own money The victim becomes the criminal in a system that was never built to protect us anyway. Now the DA and the judge want to murder me with a sentence that I can't seem to measure up. Justice is a setup, and the system is the trap They sit high in their robes, with their gavel gun on their laps.

**Only in Yonkkkers...** Where survival feels like a crime—one for all and freedom is only a rumor whispered through the cracks in the cell block walls Knowing tomorrow brings the same fight in a place

where wrong is right and the light at the end of the
tunnel is just another cop's flashlight.

**Only in Yonkkkers…** In the poor parts, the water is
dark and unclean, so you must buy a filter or a Polar
Spring. Basic human rights come with a price tag. While
they drink clean streamed water in the rich
neighborhoods and we get the dust—no cap.

**Only in Yonkkkers…** Where the streets are littered with
capsules, blue baggies, and other drug paraphernalia.
so, it can intentionally, subconsciously get you to have
an addiction, which can lead to failure. Environmental
warfare—that's their depiction. An American dream is
what Amerikkka will sell ya.

**Only in Yonkkkers…** Where they smoke dust blunts
like cigarettes and put themselves in bad predicaments
that they didn't wish. Then, they wake up the next day
not knowing what they did. There's dust, cracks, and
coke on every block. Raw, ready thots scheming on
your cheddy guap.

**Only in Yonkkkers…** They lock you up in the hospitals,
claiming that you're high—but you ain't. St. Joseph, St.
John's, St. Lawrence—all so-called wicked saints.
Where the hospital gives you ibuprofen for a gunshot,
then they discharge you quickly, say you're trespassing,
and call the cops.

**Only in Yonkkkers…** Where niggas act like crabs in the barrel, instead of keeping their eyes on the sparrow. A black cloud hangs over the hood, from North Broadway to Caryl. It's sad, though. They gentrified Getty Square and named it SOHO.

**Only in Yonkkkers…** Where the cops let the deuce heads wander free, because they're too busy engaged in institutional segregation in housing and miseducation policies. They'd rather stop you or me in the V and ask me for my ID — even if I'm just a passenger. Why do they wanna bother me?

**Only in Yonkkkers…** We are divided by blocks, street names, and hood pride. Invisible separation between the South and the North Side. While we fight for the same piece of the same pie, we never see eye to eye, because either we are too high or just don't want to see county time, from trumped-up charges, the YPD summoned. Even though you committed no crime.

**Only in Yonkkkers…** Where the system feeds on our division, where survival is the mission, and justice is just a word they use to keep us locked in their vision of a city that profits off our pain, where freedom's just a ghost, and we're all running through the rain.

# Welcome back crack

Cycle of Wrath
The era of crack is coming back (hah!)
They locked up all the black Blacks.
But we won't crack—that's a fact, fax 📠
History will 3peat itself in a splash.
Inflation has the crime
rate in a backwards bang 💥 flash
Amerikkkka still has us in a trap, crash 🪨
While watching the news, full of false facts
It will only get you confused in its warpath
(You saw that 👀 )

They're sending Fetty Wap in a swap for cash.
They pass that stash 💵
to other countries that make that fentanyl

Mexican dough powder—who are you proud of?????
It only gets louder 🗣️
They're using false pride 🦁
to generate genocide for our hides' 🐀
So, our men can try to imitate an imitation of lies.

Plagiarizing and immortalizing imaginations of the minds
Amerikkka tries to recreate greatness in its own creation
Kidnap young blacks for lab genetic mutations
I'm waiting...
They're trying to pump LGBT for US to embrace it.
But I can't take the hatred
Of Systemic racism and anti-black greatness.

They have been racially tracing me
Fingerprinting my existence, casing me
Why would they try to deface me?
Saying they love 🖤 me, but only show hatred to me
Disgracefully and distastefully 😶

But I see through the smoke screens and broken dreams
The system's schemes won't silence those screams.
We're more than the trauma they've traced

More than the history they've tried to erase
We rise from the ashes they thought would replace
So, I'm done waiting, and letting my skills go to
waste

## The New Opium

Amerikkka doesn't need to raid the poppy fields
anymore on the Middle East's soil. She doesn't
need to steal or afford the opium and the oil. The
war on drugs has cast a shadow over the black
clouds. The purest, most powerful
addiction—K2, Fentanyl—is synthetic now. It's
flowing right into our communities, in the black
crowds. A poison engineered and distributed

through the X-black files. They funded foreign wars and cherry-picked the immigrants they deem useful. Yet they sent the Haitians back—a people labeled undesirable. It cuts deep, the sight of my people wronging each other, all for entertainment. Fulfilling the cycle, doing the master's work just as Willie Lynch predicted and orchestrated. We are sleepwalking through the wreckage: some speaking the crooked word, some cutting deals with the feds, others accepting it — others neglect it. While we slumber, the neighborhood is being stripped, the block is gentrified. Outsiders claiming ground right before our eyes.

The drugs are not just what they sell on the corner; the drugs are an escape. They need something stronger than marijuana, to deal with this place. Too many choose to trade reality for the high. I know this road; I walked that path all my life. I know where it goes.
But the sleep must end. The commitment now is to the solution, the genuine one. We must actively join the revolution. The question isn't for the system; it's for us: algorithm has your

attention, Bronze feet don't rust.

What are you doing to resist these hands that exploit and manipulate our communities, mentally and economically? If you're black, you have no immunity.

# Free bee 🐝

All praise is due, but let's not act like a fool and not notice what's really happening, with these so-called free rides coming in strange packages. They rolled out these buses, right? Same old raggedy ones that have been rattling through the neighborhoods for years; paint peeling, seats worn down to the foam, but no room to stand in there. But look closer and you'll see what's new: cameras — Shiny, state-of-the-art, mounted in every corner. Watching everything, recording ya — every move. Storing every face in some database, somewhere far away being viewed.

It's a classic play, straight out of those 48 Laws of Power. You know the one that gives before they take, confection before the sour. They let people taste something sweet, get them comfortably weak, and then record their face, in plain view but discreet. Then, when summer fades and fall rolls around with its crisp air and changing leaves, that's when the prices go up at the fair, and those changes are obsolete. That's when the free ride suddenly costs more than it ever did before. They'll have all the justification they need by then, to make the score. They'll point to the increased ridership, the maintenance costs, and the security upgrades. They'll use the same playbook they've been using since forever, in every state. It's the same moves they pulled during what they called a pandemic, but what some folks saw as something more calculated.

A PLANdemic, if you will—a manufactured crisis leading to manufactured solutions. Somehow always benefit the people at the top of their movement. While everyone else pays the price, but you would benefit if you were Jewish. But here's the thing about awareness: to be aware is to be alive. To see the games being played in front of your face and to do something about it is to refuse to be jived. Too many people mistake salt for sugar these days. reaching for what they think is sweet only to get a mouthful of bitterness when the consequences hit its stage. They bite down expecting one thing and get something completely different, and then they wonder how they got played, when they shouldn't. They wonder why the taste in their mouth doesn't match what they were promised. That's like travelling to the Caribbean and expecting snow in the Bahamas.

So yes, ride the free bus everywhere. Take advantage of the freebie they share, while it's there. But let's be clear, don't let it sting your view of what's really happening. Don't let the temporary sweetness blind you to the bees waiting underneath the passion of this. Use the system, but don't let the system use you. Stay sharp. Stay questioning, never neutral. Stay aware of who benefits when you stop paying attention or pay the consequences of being ignorant of their intentions. Because at the end of the day they are pursuing. They're counting on your ignorance and confusion. They're counting on people being too tired, too distracted, or too wired for small mercies to notice the larger pattern. But once you see it, it's something that you can't unsee. Once you know the difference between salt and sugar, between coffee and tea, between genuine service and surveillance dressed up as safety—that's when you're truly free. Use don't get used. Make sure you know the rules and combinations to the wisdom's gate key.

# Chapter 4: Health, Healing & Self-Reflection

# Self-Health is Wealth

We spend our lives pouring into others—filling up their cups while ours run dry, tending to their gardens while our own soil cracks from neglect. Why?

But the most revolutionary act is turning that love inward, watering your own roots first. Your ID card carries one name, one soul. That's the main one who deserves your devotion, bro. Treat yourself, don't cheat yourself. This isn't selfish—it's survival. You will see the wealth. Self-preservation isn't just staying alive; it's thriving through the pain and saving your own life.

Manifest the best version of you, because everything you do turns back into you. Attraction starts with how you see yourself. Feed your mind the truth. Nourish it with affirmations. Health is wealth.

Stand in the mirror and declare your beauty until it's undeniable. When you look good, you feel good—so smile don't deny your soul. Let your eyes adore you. Let that smile be your rebellion against doubt. The law of attraction works both ways, you are what you think about. What you give yourself the return is multiplied. Remember what they taught us in school— "I before U." Let your goals be centrified.

The deeper lesson is this: you come first in your own story. Not out of arrogance but out of necessity, you own your own glory. The tools for success, prosperity, and joy are already in your hands. The only barrier is you— how you are perceived to be less than —your fears, your hesitation, your old stories of unworthiness, your unwillingness to understand. You were created in perfectness. Health is wealth, and wealth begins the moment you decide you are worth the investment. You are your own testament.

You've traced the maps of others, filling their voids with your own soul's light, but the compass needle now swings home, pointing to the temple you left in the night. The cracked soil waits, the garden of you, where the truest, wildest bloom must start. This turning inward is not a retreat, but the deepest work of unfolding your heart.

Let the wellspring of your being be the first to know your gentle hand. Declare the worth that needs no witness, the divine truth you already can understand. Shed the old skin of "less than," and let your perfection be the guide. You are the author, the hero, the glory—with no need to seek, recognition for it is held inside.

## Witness Fitness

Let's have a drink ☐ at my club fitness,
Come witness this synergy.
I know you've got a tendency
For booze 🍺 and white Hennessy, 🍷
But I'd rather you sip with me
Something healthy 🥥
Something full of energy, ☕
That's good for your memory 🧠
So, you can remember me, 🧑🏾
Smell me.
That's that homegrown cologne of herbs 🌿
Not that wacko tobacco 💨 step back, yo,

7,000 chemicals? That's absurd.
Instead, put these juices in your life:
Celery, mangoes, carrot sticks,
Pineapples, ginger in the blender—
Not additives, addictive tricks.
Not that fake sugar your body can't digest,
But if you must,
Add stevia or Splenda, I suggest.

Sweetheart, when you look good, you feel good.
So, start with 20 minutes on the treadmill
Do it now, while you still could.
Don't wait 'til it's too late
To try to shed the weight.
The time is now-- to elevate,
Ditch that cloned and contaminated beef
From off your plates.

And while you're at it,
Toss that pork  off your forks  ,
So, you can sharpen your thoughts.
'Cause you are what you eat.
Fast food  equals faster defeat,
Leading to cycles of pain on repeat
Remorse in your chest,
Contortions in your sleep.

Can't get off the porch or up the steps
But you've got the power
To master what you devour.
Beef takes 48 hours
Just to pass through your bowels.

Even the chicken  is a foul fowl,
Cloned and pumped with hormones and 'roids—
No wonder you're paranoid,
Popping antacids
For swollen adenoids.

Spend more time in motion
And less time on Androids.
Build habits that heal, promote it:
Let the law of attraction you can't avoid
Clean house from the first floor to the attic.
Your flaws? They've got causes, combat it
But food can be toxic
Leaving your body tragic.

So, watch what you're eating—literally.
Read the labels--visually.
Make it make sense.
Your plate is your medicine.
And never forget:

You are what you eat, sisters and brethren.

## Fast-food vulture

They straight culture-vulturing US using our slanging, but these Doritos Papadias are really banging! These fast-food corporations keep taking what we nonchalantly creating. They are profiting from our imagination. They're raking in billions, meanwhile the real Auntie Juana can't even feed her own children. They take our sauce and drip, then dip, then charge us a cost and flip the whole table over, commercializing our recipes and slogans. I'm telling you, brother—no Hulk Hogan—they won't even give us the credit when with the truth you approach them. They take your name from you, then you must buy it back to own it. They're controlling what you eat through the TVs. The ads attract you because it's already in your mental CC. It's subconsciously in your inner greed to chew, from growing up eating the same foods on the avenue. It's all about the revenue!!! Big business doesn't care about your health or your fitness... Can I get a witness? Word to Jehovah, your food isn't prayed over, so it isn't kosher. But don't be mad at me, fam, just because I'm the one that told you. I'm just His messenger, bringing the good news of what you can do, I won't hold ya. You just have to apply it with some applications and don't deny your gifts by just sitting there waiting... to get paid—that is so played!

So, wake up, my peoples! Stop feeding the machine that's feeding off you. Cook your own food, create your own wealth, and keep your culture in your own hands, tighten up your belt. Because when we control our own narrative, we control our own destiny. But fighting for your rights won't come effortlessly. I gain the best integrity when I invest in me.

# Mind Over Violence

You don't need to use guns, knives, or weapons for beef all the time. Use them only for self-defense.

Learn how to fight and use your mind, when things get intense. Especially if you already have a felony. You don't want to be dead or in prison regretting your decisions.

Penny-pinching just to get commissary.

Think twice before you react, one wrong move, you can't take it back. Your whole life's off track They got three strikes laws waiting for you to slip. One moment of anger could end your whole trip. Your kids need their father, your mama needs her son. But you're thinking with your ego instead of your gun

Violence ain't the answer to every single problem

When you got a record, the system's there to rob them of their freedom, their future, their chances to grow. Smart brothers know when

to fight and when to let go. Use your words
as weapons, your brain as your shield
Sometimes walking away is the realest thing
you can yield. Prison walls don't care one
tweet
About your reputation on the streets. They
just want another number, another defeat.
Another brown man down in hell's creek.

Another young brother locked up behind bars
trading his potential worth for some
meaningless scars. So, think before you
move, calculate your next step. Play chess,
because one bad decision is all you get. The
streets will forget you when you're locked
away. But your family will suffer-- every single
day

So, choose wisdom over warfare, knowledge
over hate. Don't let your pride determine your
fate

# Free Ya Mind

It's crazy how they put their flag 🇺🇸 on my
head
Took all of my bread 💰
Disarmed me, and tried to neuter my third leg
🦵
Tried to crack my skull 💀 like an egg 🥚
To them I was just a Blackleg
They had me plea into a pledge
But I solemnly swear to never 👎 fall off the
ledge
I rock gems that Rakim would've said
Juice's 4 life keeps me balanced and read
As I strive to hold the edge
Like I'm a bulk Hogan with a sledge
Free ya mind 🧠, free ya mind
Read the times
See the subliminal sublime
Between the lines
Open ya eyes 👀 👁
The blind can't lead the blind!!!!.

# *Chapter 5: Love, Identity & Respect*

# Your Right

You're right.
You have the right to be gay,
And I have the right to be straight.
We all have our own cross to bear
At the pearly gates.
So, who am I to judge you?
Or cast a stone at your face?
I'm far from perfect,
And I have made plenty of mistakes.
Who am I to hate you?
Because of the sexual
Preferences that you choose?
You have your own free will
To do whatever you want to do.

None of us should be hated
On personal decisions once we make it,
because at the end of the day
It's your life to live, so embrace it.
We were all born naked
Just in different forms of races,
but hatred is not the answer
towards someone else's relations.
You can do as you please
But just don't aggressively
Bring it to me,
That's all that I'm saying
Sincerely and respectfully.
So, if you love men or women
That ain't none of my businesses.
It's your decision.
You should be able to go outside
without punishment or permission.
You shouldn't be discriminated against
Or harassed verbally,
Or mistreated on purpose
Or cursed or beat.
Because at the end of the day
We are all under one sun
And to Him, I'm His son
The Almighty God,
The Judge of all judges, shalom

If you choose to be that way
I won't hate you or berate you,
I'm going to treat you with the same respect
I would treat my Aunt Rachel.
Because I wouldn't tolerate
Being treated unfairly too
Because of my racial and skin hues
Or whoever else they try to compare me to.
All I can do is pray for you
And let God make a way for you.
You have the right to be productive,
Happy and gay too.
I know how it feels to wear a target,
For I am now impartial, behold
So, I can emphasize and empathize
How you get shoulders in the subarctic cold?
I apologize if I ever criticized
Or made you feel uncomfortable.
My ignorance was viciously blatant,
I was impatient and uncontrollable.
I know how it feels to get oppressed
Because they can't accept who I am,
Nevertheless, never stress
Because you are who you are, I overstand.
I respect you as a human being,
Man or woman.
No matter the preference

Of your gender's stance is.
Being that you're one of God's children
You have the right to be loved,
To be free, and to be happy.
You have the right to choose
Who you want to be
Or who you want to marry.
I ain't Jesus
Nor will I be impetuous
And give you mistreatments
Just for the sake of God
I love you, and I mean it
You can choose to do what you want to do
With your own vagina or penis.
So, you can wave your flag with pride
I will never deny or criticize
Or be biased on how you choose to live your life
We both can relate to the hate
and the injustices in Amerikkka,
of being prejudiced against
And treated as inferior.
So, I ain't going to knock it
If you decide to come out of the closet
Or you want to stay on the down low
Because to be honest... you're right.
You have the right to live your life
the way you wanna, bro.

You can be any color in the rainbow
And shouldn't have to feel pain though...
The same goes for the confused
Do what you do but stay true.

## The A,gendas They Switch

Mi$$ Amerikkka thinks she is slick.
Man, I'm telling you, but I'm hipped
When they ask your race, gender, or etcetera
Tell 'em the opposite.
Mix it all up.
Because all that stuff is just stats
A crock of ish—a tool
for them to find new ways to discriminate,
eliminate, or hate you.

For instance,
they wanna play with this LGBT narrative.
If we can switch genders, then they can switch
agendas.
Throw all that gibberish in a blender, it's imperative.
One day they say it's okay to be gay,
To go the other way,
To be married and carried away.
But if you're in prison, how do they determine
If you're a man or a woman?
Didn't they say we have the right to choose?
So, lock me up in a women's prison then.
despite you being confused.

Don't you see how Amerikkka tries to play God
Judging men, but letting them win if they're
feminine?
How can Miss Amerikkka pick and choose
Who she views as "dudes" based on aggression or
obsession?
I guess these are the hidden lessons.
But it clearly says: Don't sleep with your brethren
As you would with a female, brethren.

Don't let their labels stick.
Break the mold and make it quick.

The only truth I speak is my freedom.
and no matter what your sexual preference is,
that ain't my business,
My goal is to lead them.

# Pre Judge

That's prejudice, to me—what they did to Nick Cannon and Kyrie. Well... I'm from the hood, that has big cannons and real weed, not potpourri. They pre-judged them, stripped their endorsements. crippled their financial capabilities, divorced them from their chips—Big Pun intended. These big businesses run behind false religions and conspiracies, always reaching into pockets that don't belong to them, literally.

What's wrong with them? They might try to Malcolm or DM--X me, but I'm Gucci in Philly FDC. I ain't no rat falling into their cheese traps, no 5K1 in my paperwork (hah!)—check the facts. They can't silence my lips because I know my First Amendment, and I know their deceits and how they are intended. Weren't these the same Pharisees that plotted to kill Jesus for speaking his peace? How can the coffee bean call the kettle black with the same mouthpiece? They talk about peace, but where's the relief? Brown men are still getting judicially slaughtered in these streets.

What about the pope who touched my little niece in Little Italy when she was only 666 weeks—literally. Sheesh. But I guess the focus ain't on the hocus-pocus feces. They threaten me as a species unless they need me. I'd rather they just leave me — be. And find something else safe to play with, my patience reached its peak. CC — The FBI, Feds, ATF, NYPD, and I.C.E—copycats. They mimic what we build, then attack us as Blacks. They give it to us, then take it back... highway robberies. They've got a problem with me because what I speak and teach doesn't fit their textbook ideologies. Sorry, I am not sorry B! There are no apologies. Stop trying to Black Rob our musicians and athletes. From college to the pros, let them get their dough. Pay them to compete. They're making pretty pennies, and these powers still doctor our legacies. They want to Bill Cosby me, and R. Kelly me—but I'm not built with that Kyrie jelly. Respectfully...

Pay these athletes a real Nike check. Don't put nooses around their necks disguised as slave-chain advances. They can't see, but you've still got the advantage in their enhancements. That math doesn't add up to me. I'm a king who plays chess, I don't eat checkers, I'm no fool. My experiences were my teachers in schools. I know the additives in fast food, and what they would do and how cruel they get if you let it get out of hand. That's the truth. That's why I get my checkups from head to toe, to

make sure everything is copacetically. So don't
mess with me. Respectfully.

## King your Dome

She's never been a leader
But she'll have you lying in her kingdom
She'll surely understand that she is not a princess
She holds her own crown
But the weight of it isn't what you think it is.
It's a reminder, not a fairy tale.
Another man down
She's a man-eater
Appetite insatiable, hunger never satisfied
She'll consume your soul before you realize
You were never dining, you were always the meal
She feeds on devotion, devours what's real
Leaves nothing but bones
and broken promises behind
A graveyard of hearts she's carefully designed

She's a Master of Game and illusions.
Mirrors and smoke, a carefully crafted confusion
You see what she wants you to see
The damsel, the dream, the fantasy
But behind the curtain, she's pulling the strings
A puppeteer of emotions, controlling everything
She'll make you believe you're the one in control

she's already mapped out
how she'll swallow you whole
She doesn't respect any Black man
Won't bow to the king; she came from
She'll use him, abuse him,
then claim he's the problem
Emasculate his pride, then wonder why he's fallen
She wants his strength but resents his struggle
hates his culture but loves his hustle

She'll take his seed but poison the root
Then blame him for the bitter fruit
She secretly wants to be white
Indirectly succumbing to Willie Lynch's hype
Divide and conquer is playing out in her mind
She internalized the hate, made it her own design

Colorism is her weapon, self-hatred is her sound
She'll bleach her skin and straighten her crown
Anything to distance herself from the Brown
The master's psychology was passed down
She's a slave to his vision, committing the crime
Against her own people, her own bloodline

Then came the fall, the spiraling reverberation
A major, unfortunate situation
illusion shattered, the mirror cracked in rotation.

Reality came crashing down with no hesitation
She hit rock bottom, alone and in the cold
All those she betrayed, all those she sold
But it was her own people who came to her aid
The Black men she disrespected,
the ones she played
They lifted her up when she had nowhere to go
Showed her the love she refused to know
And in that moment, she realized at once
She'd been bamboozled, playing the dunce
Turning against her own, while chasing a lie
Trading her soul for acceptance
that would never arrive
The very ones she rejected were the only ones real
The only ones who saw her,
the ones who could heal
Her broken spirit, her colonized mind
She'd been blind to the treasure she left behind
Now she understands the weight of that crown
It's not about ruling, it's about coming back around
To the soil she came from, the roots she denied
The community that loved her when her ego died
She's no longer a leader, no longer a queen
Just a woman rebuilding
what she'd broken and meaned
Learning to respect the Black man she scorned

Finding herself
among the people that she'd mourned
Her kingdom was empty, built on sand
But redemption begins when you finally understand
That you can't rise alone, can't conquer by hate
And some lessons only come
when it's almost too late

# A Walking Renaissance

They tried to box me in, but I broke the mold.
Like Kunta with the roots. I won't be sold
My soul ain't for auction, my thoughts are too bold.
I spit heat like furnaces in a tenement's cold
Where families huddle and stories unfold
Of struggle and triumph that never gets old
I carry the weight of the tales they told
Turning their pain into power, lead into gold

They gave me chains;
I turned them into charm links.
They tried to drown me in doubt.
I floated and did not sink.
I'm the ink in the pen that rewrites what they think.
A walking renaissance, resemblance of a Sphinx

On the edge while they try to push me to the brink
But I'm self-respected and didn't give in to the clink.
They tried to make me disappear like invisible ink.
But I'm permanent and eternal, I refuse to shrink.
I see the system glitchin'—it's a loop of oppression.
But I'm the exception. Poetry is my expression.
My essence ain't measured by your laws
or your lessons.
I'm the question they fear,
the truth they are suppressing.
The nightmare that haunts every colonial session
The answer to prayers
from every ancestor's blessing
I'm proof that their lies need constant refreshing.
'Cause I'm living, breathing, teaching, and
progressing

So, I rise like the sun through the smog
and the stress.
With a mic in my hand and a heart in my chest,
I confess I'm blessed, though they tried to finesse.
Now I manifest power in every breath
I'm writing my legacy, passing the tests
Breaking generational curses, giving God my best
To the youth who come after, may they manifest
A future where your freedom ain't just a request

# God Makes You King, Not Man

A King is more than a ring. More than a crown, more than a throne, more than the gold they flash when they want to be known. A King is a calling, not a costume. He doesn't need jewels to shine—he glows from the womb.

A King shines brighter than bling. Because his light ain't bought, it's born. It's the fire in his chest when his people mourn. It's the wisdom in his walk, the thunder in his talk. It's the way he stands firm when the world wants him to crawl.

A King leads his people. Not just with laws, but with love. Not just with power, but with purpose from above. He doesn't just reign—he rises. He doesn't just speak—he prophesies. He doesn't just rule—he remembers his people's cries. A goat and a sheep may graze the same field, but the shepherd knows the difference. The goat bucks, the sheep bows. The goat strays, the sheep stays. But the King watches both, because the crown doesn't discriminate—it elevates.

A King rules over both, with a faster gross. But his profit ain't in pockets—it's in progress. He multiplies mercy, he invests in justice. He builds wealth in wisdom and builds the strength of injustice.

A King is chosen, not crowned. Anointed like David but

hunted like Malcolm. He walks through fire like Moses, And still parts seas with his voice for a Godly outcome. He doesn't need a palace—he needs a purpose. He doesn't need a robe—he needs a reason. Not a turban. Apparel doesn't breed him.

A King knows his people are prophets. He listens to the cries of the single mothers, not the gossip. The wisdom of the elders, The fire of the youth. He doesn't just reign—he rises. And when he rises, we rise with him. So don't mistake a ring for royalty. Don't confuse bling with blessing. A real King builds kingdoms from brokenness. He Shepard's his people to freedom— Not just in body, but in spirit he leads them.

A King is the echo of ancestors. He is the drumbeat of resistance. The scripture of survival. The gospel of grit. He is the sermon and the script. The prayer and the protest. A King is the blueprint of liberation. He doesn't just wear the crown—he embraces it. He doesn't just sit on the throne; he stands in the gap. He doesn't just speak the truth; he lives it to be exact. He doesn't just fight battles—he births movements. So, when you see him, don't look for glitter, look for grace. Don't look for diamonds—look for direction. Don't look for wealth—look for wisdom. Because a King ain't what he wears— A King is what he bears.

# Chapter 6: **Tributes & Rising Through the Smoke**

# Rising Through the Smoke

Shots fired—I am not a liar. The whole empire is collapsing, sired. We need to revolt and retire, not live in these BS lies, bruh. You don't have to get high and pick your own poison. This sip is annoying. I am employed and enjoying it. yet I am under distress. I am stressed and overworked. I'm worth far more than my wor$t. I am thirsty and cursed, underdressed for this sizzling, homeless investment on Amerikkka's turf. We invest in your corporations and Incs—what do you think, I think? That's not lean in those cups, but holy spirits. Stop stringing our guitar environments and gentrifying our projects.

What happened to the summer campaigns—so
don't complain about the congestion. I cannot
change my skin, nor would it make sense to enjoy
your violent messages. Violins silence the sirens in
my environment; projects are being gentrified while
we are being fried fish.

We are outside, alive, aware of their plagues. It is
time again to pray, as THEY prey on our ways. Yet
we will not fear their dracos, or drones that are
never shown. We have chromes and chromosomes
in our homes. I am awake—and I am not alone. I do
not speak of the cannons or cobrones lurking in my
zones. My vibes are good, God willing. We will rise
and apply what God has advised, not the lies
drifting in the clouds or floating across the skies.

We will not be broken or disrespected. Their chains
are only as strong as the lies we accepted. We rise
with our minds, our hearts, our souls. armed with
truth, not guns, they fear what they can't control. We
are guided by spirit, not oppression. They may try to
steal our reflection. But our worth, our dreams, they
cannot steal our vision. Even if they try to give US
life in prison. We stand awake, aware, and
unshaken. The empire falls, but we endure and

embrace it. And when the smoke clears, we will still be here, breathing, building, rising—without fear.

# Cruising to Cruizer

Tonight, I'm lighting up a fat blunt for my bro, hah!
We went way back, like Maybach seats laid back.
From Sleepy Hollow to Y.O., lifetime in our stride,
You may be gone, but you're still here in my mind.

Forever my friend, forever my kin,
Every bar I write, you're alive within.
Rest easy, Cruiser — Dwayne Dixon,
Your name still rings, your spirit still glistens.
We used to kick it and chase chicks,
Young kings with big dreams, taking life in sprints.
Now you're gone forever, I can't understand,
Why did the Father take you early from our hands?

You stayed fly even high as the moon,
Pain in my chest, but I turn it into a tune.
A poem to cry for you, to celebrate your energy
You dancing in school burned into my memory

Tracks we never made, ideas that we had
You'd sing; I'd rap
that dream never came to pass
Your pure talent, the world won't get to fully hear
But Rob is gonna carry your name, no fears.

The memories we made, the honeys we laid,
The money we gave away,
chasing highs that strayed.
Cruising up those blocks, hollering at thots,
Fearless and young, always at those spots.

You sang and danced, inspired my rhymes,
Now I write these stanzas to honor your shine.
I saw your photos, thought you were still here,
Hit me hard, brought my eyes to tears.
Life is fragile, time precious and rare,
Your loss made me see what we had, right there.

Part of me still hopes you'll walk through that door,
Big smile on your face, another story, like before.
But my heart knows the truth, no miracle comes,
This world took another brother, leaving me numb.
More than a friend, you were family, kid,
And everything I do is for how we lived.
Forever in my heart, forever in my pen,
I'll live enough life for the both of us — Amen.

# About Author

Coolgmack is a voice forged in the concrete jungles of Westchester and NYC, a poet who turned **pain into purpose**. After graduating from Sleepy Hollow High, his path led him through Rikers Island, an experience that sharpened his words into weapons of truth.

Though he is still serving an **unjust, perpetual sentence** from a crime committed 20 years ago that carried only a 10-year term, Coolgmack does not let that deter him. From behind bars, he channels the grit of survival and the ache of injustice into his work. Poetry remains his sanctuary, his megaphone, and his redemption, fueling his fight against **injustices in Amerikkka**.

Coolgmack is an author, publisher, and entrepreneur on a mission to spark a revolution through revelation, helping communities uncover their inner strength. His latest work, including **"poetic injustices in Amerikkka,"** is a testament to the holy fusion of pain, passion, and purpose.

Find him everywhere the ink spills—on all social media platforms, including **TikTok, YouTube, Twitter, and Instagram,** where he is universally known as **@coolgmack**, or visit his website at **coolgmack.com**.

# More books by Coolgmack

Find all these titles on amazon.com
coolgmack.com   etc.

"POETIC INJUSTICE$ IN AMERIKKKA" by Coolgmack is a powerful lyrical analysis of systemic racism in America. This thought-provoking work provides firsthand insight into institutional racism while advocating for economic and social restitution for Black Americans. examines historical oppression and its impact on current socioeconomic structures, race relations, and politics. He argues for changing the rules of economic opportunity so everyone has a fair chance to succeed. Drawing from multigenerational community experiences, he passes down ancestral wisdom and survival strategies, reminding his people they are enough and encouraging them to choose life beyond pain and trauma.

offers a raw and unfiltered look at the complexities of love. In this powerful collection, he navigates the tumultuous journey from **heartbreak and betrayal** to the unwavering pursuit of a love that is true and lasting. *Sucker4Love* is a testament to the pain and triumph of human connection. With a voice that is both vulnerable and resilient, Coolgmack exposes the deep scars of past relationships while holding onto the hope for a future defined by genuine intimacy and devotion.

This is a book for anyone who has ever been a **"sucker for love"**—who has given their all and lost, only to rise again with a stronger belief in the power of an honest heart

**Sucker4love Too**: "Love Ain't Logical its lyrical" is a soul-baring collection of poetry from coolgmack that navigates the intricate dance of love, loss, and self-discovery. The author invites you into his world, where heartfelt verses are a testament to his journey. He grapples with the absence of a father he never knew while finding guidance in his spiritual legacy. He confronts past mistakes and addiction, offering a profound apology to his mother that resonates with raw honesty. The collection delves deep into the tumultuous landscape of romantic love—from the dizzying highs of a "flawless" romance to the agonizing lows of a broken heart. Through poems that are both vulnerable and resilient, the author explores the challenges of trusting again and the hope that persists even after disappointment. Sucker4love Too is more than just poetry; it's a powerful narrative of resilience, a tribute to the enduring power of love, and a beacon for anyone seeking to find their way back to themselves.

Psalms in My Palms is a collection of heartfelt psalms, prayers, and poetic reflections born out of seasons of pain, redemption, and unshakable faith. Drawing from his personal journey through hardship, incarceration, and spiritual renewal, Coolgmack—offers words that meet readers in their darkest valleys and guide them toward God's light. Each piece blends lyrical beauty with scriptural truth, speaking to those who feel broken, oppressed, or forgotten. Within these pages are declarations of gratitude, prayers for strength and deliverance, and poetic portraits of God's unchanging love.

More than a book of poems, this is a devotional companion—a sacred space where you can pause, reflect, and write your own prayers in response. Psalms in My Palms is for anyone longing to be reminded that they are seen, chosen, and never alone. Whether rejoicing on the mountaintop or enduring a storm, you'll find words here to anchor your heart and lift your spirit.

**Chronicles of a Hangry Black Soul** is a raw, unapologetic poetry collection documenting a life hungry for truth, justice, and spiritual liberation. Through unfiltered verses, the author confronts systemic injustice, personal struggle, and the journey toward healing. The collection explores: **Social & Spiritual Commentary**: Exposing a "rigged" world of scams and fake love while offering a mirror for self-discovery and a guide through modern chaos. **The Prison System**: Raw testimony of dehumanization and isolation, where freedom is elusive and the system reduces public defenders to jokes. **Relationships & Loyalty**: Examining betrayal by fair-weather friends and celebrating the "Day Ones" who remained loyal through adversity. **Healing & Transformation**: Chronicling evolution from the "drug game" to "Elevation Season"—rising spiritually, mentally, and financially to build a new kingdom with divine wisdom.

**Sucker4drugs** chronicles the journey through addiction, despair, and recovery, exploring substance abuse, violence, incarceration, and redemption through raw street experiences. The **Destructive Cycle** Early poems depict the devastating effects of drug use, particularly PCP. Characters like "Dirty Diana" and "Derek" illustrate addiction's physical and emotional toll—paranoia, violence, incarceration, and betrayal.. **Personal Struggle** Poems delve into loneliness, desperation, and internal conflict, portraying the relentless grip drugs have on mind and spirit. Recovery **and Hope** Amidst darkness, the collection offers messages of hope, encouraging honesty, faith, and spiritual growth as tools for healing. The **Healing Journey** The

"Day One" through "Day 28" series intimately documents recovery's daily struggles—confronting temptation, rebuilding life, and finding resilience.

**Identity and Purpose** Poems explore self-discovery and reclaiming purpose, emphasizing that circumstances refine rather than define us.

They say love doesn't cost a thing—but for him, it costs everything. Sucker4Pain is a gritty, uncut testimony from a man who gave his all to the wrong women and nearly lost himself in the process. This ain't no love story—it's a survival story. Its raw pain served cold, dressed in designer lies and false promises. Through a poetic fusion of heartbreak, prison reflections, betrayal, addiction, and faith, this powerful collection gives voice to everyone who's ever been played, betrayed, locked up, or left behind. Told in vivid street verses and emotional confessionals, this book is more than poetry—it's a purge. A spiritual detox from toxic love and generational curses. From being set up and stripped down, to finding strength in the ruins, Sucker4Pain captures the real-life struggle of trusting the wrong women and finding God on the other side of grief.If you've ever been hurt, hustled, or hardened by love—you'll feel this in your soul.

**Sucker4Lust** is a collection of erotic poetry that delves into the raw, uninhibited world of desire and passion. The book is a journey through lust, presented through two distinct perspectives—that of a young, confident man consumed by his hunger, and women drawn to his intense charisma. The poems, which are at times witty, provocative, and tender, follow a narrative arc. They begin with an introduction to a world where lust is not a sin but a form of salvation. The stories then unfold through the eyes of a character known as "Mr. Thriller," a seductive and unapologetic figure who navigates his desires with a captivating swagger. His verses are direct and sensual, celebrating the thrill of a physical connection. The collection also includes a female point of view, exploring the intoxicating pull of this "magnetic space" and the surrender to a "willing death" of passion. The book concludes with an "Aftermath" section, where the focus shifts from a purely physical connection to a deeper, more lasting bond, suggesting that lust, when fully explored, can evolve into something more profound. Ultimately, Sucker 4 Lust is a poetic exploration of the body's truth and the soul's temptation.

This unique collection of poetry is a walk in the world of SlowMotion.the author/poet  Relatable situations. Loving words. Takes you to a place of a hurting heart, overcoming pain. Bravery and boldness to rebuild. Poems about Mending Hearts. Coming together and finding understanding.I'm excited for the world to read my words.I want to show the world that it is possible to live out your wonderful dreams positively. Keep dreaming Big

..This unique collection of poetry is a walk in the world of SlowMotion.Relatable situations.Loving words. Takes you to a place of a hurting heart, overcoming pain. Bravery and boldness to rebuild. Poems about Mending Hearts. Coming together and finding understanding